The Case for the Resurrection

NEW INTERNATIONAL VERSION

THE CASE FOR

THE

RESURRECTION

**A FIRST-CENTURY REPORTER
INVESTIGATES THE STORY OF THE CROSS**

LEE STROBEL

Featuring notes and commentary on the Gospel of Luke from
THE CASE FOR CHRIST STUDY BIBLE

ZONDERVAN®

Library of Congress Catalog Card Number 2009942295

TABLE OF CONTENTS

PART

ONE

MY JOURNEY INTO THE EVIDENCE

It didn't take long for me to conclude that the truth or falsity of all world religions — and the ultimate meaning of life itself — come down to just one key issue: did Jesus, or did he not, return from the dead? The answer to that fundamental question would settle everything.

For much of my life, I was an atheist. I determined at a young age that God didn't create people, but that people created God. Fearful of death, they invented in regards to a benevolent deity and a blissful heaven to give them the illusion of hope. The mere idea of an all-powerful, all-knowing, all-loving Creator of the universe seemed so absurd to me that it wasn't even worth my time to check it out.

Granted, I tend to be a skeptic. My education is in journalism and law, and for years I served as the legal editor of *The Chicago Tribune,* where we prided ourselves on our skepticism. We didn't take anyone's word at face value, instead preferring to get at least two sources to confirm a fact before we printed it in the paper. One of my colleagues actually had a sign in his cubicle that reflected our cynicism: "If your mother says she loves you — check it out!"

Without an overarching moral framework for my life, I made up my morality as I went. My main value was to bring maximum pleasure to myself. As a result — and this is difficult for me to admit — I lived a very immoral, drunken, profane, narcissistic and even self-destructive life.

I had a lot of anger inside of me. If you had asked me back then why I was so mad, I don't think I could have explained it. But looking back, I can see that I was always after the perfect high and the ultimate experience of pleasure. But in the end, everything would end in bitter disappointment.

All too often this anger would bubble to the surface. I remember getting into an argument with my wife Leslie. In a fit of raw rage, I reared back and kicked a hole right through our living room wall. My wrath left both her and our little daughter, Alison, in tears.

In fact, I'll tell you the ugliest thing about me: when Alison was a toddler, if she was playing alone with some toys in the living room and heard me come home from work through the front door, her natural reaction would be to simply gather her toys, go into her room and close the door. She must have thought, *Is he going to be drunk again? Is he going to be kicking holes in the wall? At least it's nice and quiet in here.* Much to my embarrassment, that sums up who I was.

The key to everything

One afternoon, Leslie rocked our marriage by announcing that after a period of spiritual searching she had decided to become a follower of Jesus. I expected the worst, but in the ensuing months I began to see positive changes in her character and values. Finally, when she invited me to go with her to church one Sunday, I decided to go — partly because I was impressed by the changes I saw in her and partly because I hoped that I might be able to get her out of this cult that she was getting entangled in.

Pastor Bill Hybels' message that morning, aptly titled *Basic Christianity*, stunned me by shattering so many of my misconceptions about the faith. Thoroughly intrigued, I decided to use my journalism and legal training to systematically investigate whether there was credibility to any religion — especially Christianity. This launched me into what turned out to be a nearly two-year spiritual quest.

It didn't take long for me to conclude that the truth or falsity of all world religions — and the ultimate meaning of life itself — comes down to just one key issue: did Jesus, or did he not, return from the dead? The answer to that fundamental question would settle everything.

Why? Because Jesus claimed to be the unique Son of God. Even in the earliest biography written about him, the Gospel of Mark, which is based on the eyewitness accounts of the disciple Peter, Jesus calls himself the Son of Man. This was a reference to Daniel 7:13 – 14, in which the Son of Man has divine attributes. He is in the very presence of the Father; he has authority, glory and sovereign power; he is worshiped by all nations; and he will come at the end of the world to judge humankind and rule forever. In other words, the claim to being the Son of Man is, in effect, a claim to divinity.

In John 10:30, Jesus declares, "I and the Father are one," meaning "one in essence." How did members of the crowd interpret what he was saying? They picked up stones to kill him "for blasphemy, because you, a mere man, claim to be God" (John 10:33).

Ultimately, the high priest asked Jesus point-blank: "Are you the Christ, the Son of the Blessed One?" (Mark 14:61). The first two words out of Jesus' mouth were unambiguous: "I am." He was declared guilty of blasphemy, again because he was claiming to be divine.

Yet think about this: anyone could make such a claim of divinity — even me. The real question is whether this assertion can be backed up. However, if Jesus not only claimed to be divine, but then he also returned from the dead after three days in a tomb — well, that would be pretty convincing evidence that he was telling the truth!

In other words, rising from the dead would validate Jesus' proclamation of his divinity. This explains why the resurrection is the centerpiece of the Christian faith. As the apostle Paul said in 1 Corinthians 15:17: "And if Christ has not been raised, your faith is futile; you are still in your sins."

In short, if the resurrection is false, then Christianity is refuted. But if it's true, then regardless of what any world religion teaches, Jesus is the one-and-only Son of God. *And that changes everything.*

First-century investigative reporter

As I launched my spiritual investigation, I realized that the New Testament — based on eyewitness accounts and written during the first century when Jesus lived — would provide valuable information. While I wasn't prepared to accept these writings as being divinely inspired, I was forced to evaluate them for what they undeniably are: A set of ancient historical documents. And I knew that just as historians investigate the reliability of such ancient writers as Josephus and Tacitus, they can also use the same techniques to assess the trustworthiness of the Gospels and the rest of the New Testament accounts.

I was particularly intrigued by the writings of Luke, who penned one-quarter of the New Testament, including the Gospel that bears his name and the book of Acts. A physician and companion of the apostle Paul, Luke was sort of a first-century investigative reporter, who apparently interviewed witnesses and participants as he painstakingly pieced together what transpired with regard to the life, teachings, miracles, death and resurrection of Jesus. As a journalist, I especially liked the way Luke begins his Gospel:

Many have undertaken to draw up an account of the things that have been fulfilled among us, just as they were handed down to us by those who from the first were eyewitnesses and servants of the word. Therefore, since I myself have carefully investigated everything from the beginning, it seemed good also to me to write an orderly account for you, most excellent Theophilus, so that you may know the certainty of the things you have been taught.[1]

"The general consensus of both liberal and conservative scholars is that Luke is very accurate as a historian," I was told by Dr. John McRay, who earned his doctorate at the University of Chicago and wrote the respected textbook *Archaeology and the New Testament.*

"He's erudite, he's eloquent, his Greek approaches classical quality, he writes as an educated man and archaeological discoveries are showing over and over again that Luke is accurate in what he has to say."

In fact, there have been several instances in which scholars initially dismissed Luke as being inaccurate in a specific reference, only to have later discoveries confirm that he was correct in what he wrote.

For instance, Luke 3:1 refers to Lysanias as being the tetrarch of Abilene in about A.D. 27. For years scholars pointed to this as evidence that Luke didn't know what he was talking about, since Lysanias was the ruler of Chalcis half a century earlier.

That's when archaeology confirmed the truth of the matter. "An inscription was later found from the time of Tiberius, from A.D. 14 to 37, which names Lysanias as tetrarch of Abila near Damascus — just as Luke had written," McRay explained. "It turned out there had been two government officials named Lysanias! Once more Luke was shown to be exactly right."

One study examined Luke's references to 32 countries, 54 cities and nine islands and didn't find a single mistake, prompting one book on the topic to conclude: "If Luke was so painstakingly accurate in his historical reporting, on what logical basis may we assume he was credulous or inaccurate in his reporting of matters that were far more important, not only to him but to others as well?"[2]

Matters, for example, such as the resurrection of Jesus, which Luke says was firmly established by "many convincing proofs" (Acts 1:3).

Are you as intrigued as I was by what Luke has to say about the resurrection? Who wouldn't be curious about his "orderly account" of "the certainty of things" that he says occurred in the first century?

I've recently completed *The Case for Christ Study Bible*, which includes hundreds of notes and articles that provide context, background and explanation for what is recorded in the Old and New Testaments. What follows is an excerpt from *The Case for Christ Study Bible*, featuring the three chapters of Luke's Gospel in which he reports on Jesus' crucifixion and resurrection.[3]

Read carefully his fascinating account of the pivotal event of history that promises to change everything.

Notes

1. Luke 1:1–4

2. John Ankerberg and John Weldon, *Reading with an Answer* (Eugene, OR: Harvest House, 1997), 272.

3. See: *The Case for Christ Study Bible* (Grand Rapids, MI: Zondervan, 2009). The excerpt in this book includes articles that the study Bible features in the Gospel of Luke as well as some articles featured in the other Gospels.

PART
TWO

LUKE'S ACCOUNT OF THE DEATH AND RESURRECTION OF JESUS

Luke 22:1–71; 23:1–56; 24:1–53

AUTHOR
Luke, a Gentile physician and missionary companion of Paul

AUDIENCE
Addressed to Theophilus, but intended for all believers

DATE
Between the sixties and eighties A.D.

SETTING
Luke may have written his Gospel from Rome, though Caesarea, Achaia and Ephesus have also been suggested.

Judas Agrees to Betray Jesus

22 Now the Feast of Unleavened Bread, called the Passover, was approaching, ²and the chief priests and the teachers of the law were looking for some way to get rid of Jesus, for they were afraid of the people. ³Then Satan entered Judas, called Iscariot, one of the Twelve. ⁴And Judas went to the chief priests and the officers of the temple guard and discussed with them how he might betray Jesus. ⁵They were delighted and agreed to give him money. ⁶He consented, and watched for an opportunity to hand Jesus over to them when no crowd was present.

The Last Supper

⁷Then came the day of Unleavened Bread on which the Passover lamb had to be sacrificed. ⁸Jesus sent Peter and John, saying, "Go and make preparations for us to eat the Passover."

⁹"Where do you want us to prepare for it?" they asked.

¹⁰He replied, "As you enter the city, a man carrying a jar of water will meet you. Follow him to the house that he enters, ¹¹and say to the owner of the house, 'The Teacher asks: Where is the guest room, where I may eat the Passover with my disciples?' ¹²He will show you a large upper

room, all furnished. Make preparations there."

¹³ They left and found things just as Jesus had told them. So they prepared the Passover.

¹⁴ When the hour came, Jesus and his apostles reclined at the table. ¹⁵ And he said to them, "I have eagerly desired to eat this Passover with you before I suffer. ¹⁶ For I tell you, I will not eat it again until it finds fulfillment in the kingdom of God."

¹⁷ After taking the cup, he gave thanks and said, "Take this and divide it among you. ¹⁸ For I tell you I will not drink again of the fruit of the vine until the kingdom of God comes."

¹⁹ And he took bread, gave thanks and broke it, and gave it to them, saying, "This is my body given for you; do this in remembrance of me."

²⁰ In the same way, after the supper he took the cup, saying, "This cup is the new covenant in my blood, which is poured out for you. ²¹ But the hand of him who is going to betray me is with mine on the table. ²² The

Son of Man will go as it has been decreed, but woe to that man who betrays him." ²³ They began to question among themselves which of them it might be who would do this.

²⁴ Also a dispute arose among them as to which of them was considered to be greatest. ²⁵ Jesus said to them, "The kings of the Gentiles lord it over them; and those who exercise authority over them call themselves Benefactors. ²⁶ But you are not to be like that. Instead, the greatest among you should be like the youngest, and the one who rules like the one who serves. ²⁷ For who is greater, the one who is at the table or the one who serves? Is it not the one who is at the table? But I am among you as one who serves. ²⁸ You are those who have stood by me in my trials. ²⁹ And I confer on you a kingdom, just as my Father conferred one on me, ³⁰ so that you may eat and drink at my table in my kingdom and sit on thrones, judging the twelve tribes of Israel.

³¹ "Simon, Simon, Satan has asked to sift you*a* as wheat. ³² But I have prayed for you, Simon, that your faith may not fail. And

a 31 The Greek is plural.

22:16 *until it finds fulfillment.* Jesus yearned to keep this Passover with his disciples because it was the last occasion before he himself was to be slain as the perfect "Passover lamb" (1Co 5:7) and thus fulfill this sacrifice for all time. Jesus would eat no more Passover meals until the coming of the future kingdom. After this he will renew fellowship with those who through the ages have commemorated the Lord's Supper. Finally the fellowship will be consummated in the great Messianic "wedding supper of the Lamb" to come (Rev 19:9).
22:19 *is.* Represents or signifies. *given for you.* Anticipating his substitutionary sacrifice on the cross. *in remembrance of me.* Just as the Passover was a constant reminder and proclamation

of God's redemption of Israel from bondage in Egypt, so the keeping of Christ's command would be a remembering and proclaiming of the deliverance of believers from the bondage of sin through Christ's atoning work on the cross.
22:20 *new covenant.* Promised through the prophet Jeremiah (see 31:31 – 34) — the fuller administration of God's saving grace, founded on and sealed by the death of Jesus ("in my blood").
22:29 *confer on you a kingdom.* The following context (v. 30) indicates that this kingdom is the future form of the kingdom.
22:30 *sit on thrones.* As they shared in Jesus' trials, so they will share in his rule (see 2Ti 2:12). *judging.* Leading or ruling.

when you have turned back, strengthen your brothers."

³³But he replied, "Lord, I am ready to go with you to prison and to death."

³⁴Jesus answered, "I tell you, Peter, before the rooster crows today, you will deny three times that you know me."

³⁵Then Jesus asked them, "When I sent

WHAT'S THE MEANING OF LIFE?

THE CASE FOR
FAITH
LUKE 22:14–20

Christianity's greatest contribution to humankind is the "good news," or the gospel. This central message of the Bible portrays God's love for us, which

> In the same way, after the supper he took the cup, saying, "This cup is the new covenant in my blood, which is poured out for you."
>
> — LUKE 22:20

prompted our redemption through the shedding of Jesus' blood. Finally, once and for all, he dealt with the issues of our guilt, our loneliness and our alienation from God. Through his atoning death and resurrection, he opened up heaven for everyone who follows him.

With this truth, Christianity provides a revelation as to the meaning of life. Without that revelation, it's very difficult to have any sense of life's meaning. You end up like Albert Camus, who said in the opening paragraph of *The Myth of Sisyphus*, "Why should I or anyone not commit suicide?"

In short, Christianity explains why not. Because of God's profound love for us, as shown by Jesus' death on the cross as he willingly paid the penalty of our sin so we could be set free, we are able to relate to him and others in a healthy and deeply meaningful way.

— Adapted from interview with Dr. John D. Woodbridge

you without purse, bag or sandals, did you lack anything?"

"Nothing," they answered.

[36] He said to them, "But now if you have a purse, take it, and also a bag; and if you don't have a sword, sell your cloak and buy one. [37] It is written: 'And he was numbered with the transgressors'[a]; and I tell you that

[a] 37 Isaiah 53:12

22:37 *numbered with the transgressors.* Jesus was soon to be arrested as a criminal, in fulfillment of prophetic Scripture, and his disciples would also be in danger for being his followers.

IS IT POSSIBLE TO SWEAT DROPS OF BLOOD?

CASE NO. 42022039

THE CASE FOR
THE BIBLE

LUKE 22:39–44

The Gospel of Luke tells us that during Jesus' anguish just before his arrest, his sweat became "like drops of blood falling to the

> Being in anguish, he prayed more earnestly, and his sweat was like drops of blood falling to the ground.
>
> — LUKE 22:44

ground." Though Luke the physician may have simply meant that Jesus was perspiring so profusely that it looked like blood dripping from a wound, is it possible that Jesus was literally sweating blood?

Medical doctor and Biblical scholar Dr. Alexander Metherell says, yes, it is possible. "This is a known medical condition called hematidrosis," he says. "It's not very common, but it is associated with a high degree of psychological stress. What happens is that severe anxiety causes the release of chemicals that break down the capillaries in the sweat glands. As a result, there's a small amount of bleeding into these glands, and the sweat comes out tinged with blood. We're not talking about a lot of blood; it's just a very, very small amount."

— Adapted from interview with Dr. Alexander Metherell

this must be fulfilled in me. Yes, what is written about me is reaching its fulfillment."

38 The disciples said, "See, Lord, here are two swords."

"That is enough," he replied.

Jesus Prays on the Mount of Olives

39 Jesus went out as usual to the Mount of Olives, and his disciples followed him. **40** On reaching the place, he said to them, "Pray that you will not fall into temptation." **41** He withdrew about a stone's throw beyond them, knelt down and prayed, **42** "Father, if you are willing, take this cup from me; yet not my will, but yours be done." **43** An angel from heaven appeared to him and strengthened him. **44** And being in anguish, he prayed more earnestly, and his sweat was like drops of blood falling to the ground.*a*

45 When he rose from prayer and went back to the disciples, he found them asleep, exhausted from sorrow. **46** "Why are you sleeping?" he asked them. "Get up and pray so that you will not fall into temptation."

Jesus Arrested

47 While he was still speaking a crowd came up, and the man who was called Judas, one of the Twelve, was leading them. He approached Jesus to kiss him, **48** but

Jesus asked him, "Judas, are you betraying the Son of Man with a kiss?"

49 When Jesus' followers saw what was going to happen, they said, "Lord, should we strike with our swords?" **50** And one of them struck the servant of the high priest, cutting off his right ear.

51 But Jesus answered, "No more of this!" And he touched the man's ear and healed him.

52 Then Jesus said to the chief priests, the officers of the temple guard, and the elders, who had come for him, "Am I leading a rebellion, that you have come with swords and clubs? **53** Every day I was with you in the temple courts, and you did not lay a hand on me. But this is your hour — when darkness reigns."

Peter Disowns Jesus

54 Then seizing him, they led him away and took him into the house of the high priest. Peter followed at a distance. **55** But when they had kindled a fire in the middle of the courtyard and had sat down together, Peter sat down with them. **56** A servant girl saw him seated there in the firelight. She looked closely at him and said, "This man was with him."

57 But he denied it. "Woman, I don't know him," he said.

58 A little later someone else saw him and said, "You also are one of them."

---

a 44 Some early manuscripts do not have verses 43 and 44.

22:42 *if you are willing.* Notably, not "if you can." *this cup.* The cup of suffering (see Mt 20:22; Mk 14:36; cf. Isa 51:17; Eze 23:31).

"Man, I am not!" Peter replied.

⁵⁹About an hour later another asserted, "Certainly this fellow was with him, for he is a Galilean."

⁶⁰Peter replied, "Man, I don't know what you're talking about!" Just as he was speaking, the rooster crowed. ⁶¹The Lord turned and looked straight at Peter. Then Peter remembered the word the Lord had spoken to him: "Before the rooster crows today, you will disown me three times." ⁶²And he went outside and wept bitterly.

The Guards Mock Jesus

⁶³The men who were guarding Jesus began mocking and beating him. ⁶⁴They blindfolded him and demanded, "Proph-

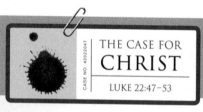

WHY WOULD JESUS WILLINGLY GO TO HIS DEATH?

THE CASE FOR
CHRIST
LUKE 22:47–53

CASE NO 42022047

Jesus intentionally walked into the arms of his betrayer, without resisting arrest. He didn't defend himself at his trial but willingly subjected himself to humiliating and agonizing forms of torture. What could possibly have motivated a person—especially an innocent one—to agree to endure this sort of punishment?

Then Jesus said to the chief priests, the officers of the temple guard, and the elders, who had come for him, "Am I leading a rebellion, that you have come with swords and clubs? Every day I was with you in the temple courts, and you did not lay a hand on me. But this is your hour—when darkness reigns."

— LUKE 22:52 - 53

Jesus knew what was coming and was willing to go through the pain because this was the only way he could redeem us—by serving as our substitute and paying the death penalty that we deserve due to our rebellion against God. That was his whole mission in coming to Earth. So when you ask what motivated him, the answer can be summed up in one word—*love*.

—Adapted from interview with Dr. Alexander Metherell

esy! Who hit you?" [65] And they said many other insulting things to him.

Jesus Before Pilate and Herod

[66] At daybreak the council of the elders of the people, both the chief priests and teachers of the law, met together, and Jesus was led before them. [67] "If you are the Christ,[a]" they said, "tell us."

Jesus answered, "If I tell you, you will not believe me, [68] and if I asked you, you would not answer. [69] But from now on, the Son of Man will be seated at the right hand of the mighty God."

[70] They all asked, "Are you then the Son of God?"

He replied, "You are right in saying I am."

[71] Then they said, "Why do we need any more testimony? We have heard it from his own lips."

23 Then the whole assembly rose and led him off to Pilate. [2] And they began to accuse him, saying, "We have found this man subverting our nation. He opposes payment of taxes to Caesar and claims to be Christ,[b] a king."

[3] So Pilate asked Jesus, "Are you the king of the Jews?"

"Yes, it is as you say," Jesus replied.

[4] Then Pilate announced to the chief priests and the crowd, "I find no basis for a charge against this man."

[5] But they insisted, "He stirs up the people all over Judea[c] by his teaching. He started in Galilee and has come all the way here."

[6] On hearing this, Pilate asked if the man was a Galilean. [7] When he learned that Jesus was under Herod's jurisdiction, he sent him to Herod, who was also in Jerusalem at that time.

[8] When Herod saw Jesus, he was greatly pleased, because for a long time he had been wanting to see him. From what he had heard about him, he hoped to see him perform some miracle. [9] He plied him with many questions, but Jesus gave him no answer. [10] The chief priests and the teachers of the law were standing there, vehemently accusing him. [11] Then Herod and his soldiers ridiculed and mocked him. Dressing him in an elegant robe, they sent him back to Pilate. [12] That day Herod and Pilate became friends — before this they had been enemies.

[13] Pilate called together the chief priests, the rulers and the people, [14] and said to them, "You brought me this man as one who was inciting the people to rebellion. I have examined him in your presence and have found no basis for your charges against him.

---

[a] 67 Or *Messiah*   [b] 2 Or *Messiah*; also in verses 35 and 39   [c] 5 Or *over the land of the Jews*

22:71 *We have heard it.* The reaction to Jesus' reply makes clear that his answer was a strong affirmative. Mark has simply, "I am" (Mk 14:62). It was blasphemy to claim to be the Messiah and the Son of God—unless, of course, the claim was true.
23:2 *subverting our nation.* Large crowds followed Jesus, but he was not misleading them or turning them against Rome. *opposes payment of taxes.* Another untrue charge (see 20:25). *claims to be Christ, a king.* Jesus claimed to be the Messiah, but not a political or military king, the kind Rome would be anxious to eliminate.

¹⁵Neither has Herod, for he sent him back to us; as you can see, he has done nothing to deserve death. ¹⁶Therefore, I will punish him and then release him.ᵃ"

¹⁸With one voice they cried out, "Away with this man! Release Barabbas to us!" ¹⁹(Barabbas had been thrown into prison for an insurrection in the city, and for murder.)

ᵃ 16 Some manuscripts him." ¹⁷Now he was obliged to release one man to them at the Feast.

IS THE DARKNESS AT JESUS' CRUCIFIXION A LITERAL REFERENCE?

One of the most problematic references in the New Testament is the claim by the Gospel writers that the earth went dark during part of the time that Jesus hung on the cross. Wasn't this merely a literary device to stress the significance of the crucifixion, rather than a reference to an actual historical occurrence? After all, if darkness had fallen over the earth, wouldn't there be at least some mention of this extraordinary event outside the Bible?

Dr. Gary Habermas, one of the world's leading experts on the resurrection, has reported on a historian named Thallus, who in A.D. 52 wrote a history of the eastern Mediterranean world since the Trojan War. Although Thallus's work has been lost, it was quoted by Julius Africanus in about A.D. 221—and it made reference to the darkness written about in the Gospels!

Explains historian Dr. Edwin M. Yamauchi, "In this passage Julius Africanus says, 'Thallus, in the third book of his histories, explains away the darkness as an eclipse of the sun—unreasonably, as it seems to me.'

"So Thallus apparently was saying, yes, there had been darkness at the time of the crucifixion, and he speculated it had been caused by an eclipse. Africanus then argues that it couldn't have

20 Wanting to release Jesus, Pilate appealed to them again. 21 But they kept shouting, "Crucify him! Crucify him!"

22 For the third time he spoke to them: "Why? What crime has this man committed? I have found in him no grounds for the death penalty. Therefore I will have him punished and then release him."

23 But with loud shouts they insistently demanded that he be crucified, and their shouts prevailed. 24 So Pilate decided to grant their demand. 25 He released the man

THE CASE FOR
THE BIBLE

LUKE 23:44–45

CASE NO. 42023044

been an eclipse, given when the crucifixion occurred."

Historian Dr. Paul Maier says this about the darkness in a footnote in his 1968 book *Pontius Pilate*:

> It was now about the sixth hour, and darkness came over the whole land until the ninth hour, for the sun stopped shining.
>
> — LUKE 23:44 - 45

This phenomenon, evidently, was visible in Rome, Athens, and other Mediterranean cities. According to Tertullian ... it was a "cosmic" or "world event." Phlegon, a Greek author from Caria writing a chronology soon after 137 A.D., reported that in the fourth year of the 202nd Olympiad (i.e., 33 A.D.) there was "the greatest eclipse of the sun" and that "it became night in the sixth hour of the day [i.e., noon] so that stars even appeared in the heavens. There was a great earthquake in Bithynia, and many things were overturned in Nicaea."

Yamauchi concludes, "So there is, as Paul Maier points out, nonbiblical attestation of the darkness that occurred at the time of Jesus' crucifixion. Apparently, some found the need to try to give it a natural explanation by saying it was an eclipse."

— Adapted from interview with Dr. Edwin M. Yamauchi

who had been thrown into prison for insurrection and murder, the one they asked for, and surrendered Jesus to their will.

The Crucifixion

26 As they led him away, they seized Simon from Cyrene, who was on his way in from the country, and put the cross on him and made him carry it behind Jesus. 27 A large number of people followed him, including women who mourned and wailed for him. 28 Jesus turned and said to them, "Daughters of Jerusalem, do not weep for me; weep for yourselves and for your children. 29 For the time will come when you will say, 'Blessed are the barren women, the wombs that never bore and the breasts that never nursed!' 30 Then

> " 'they will say to the mountains, "Fall on us!"
> and to the hills, "Cover us!" ' a

31 For if men do these things when the tree is green, what will happen when it is dry?"

32 Two other men, both criminals, were also led out with him to be executed. 33 When they came to the place called the Skull, there they crucified him, along with the criminals — one on his right, the other on his left. 34 Jesus said, "Father, forgive them, for they do not know what they are doing." b And they divided up his clothes by casting lots.

35 The people stood watching, and the rulers even sneered at him. They said, "He saved others; let him save himself if he is the Christ of God, the Chosen One."

36 The soldiers also came up and mocked him. They offered him wine vinegar 37 and said, "If you are the king of the Jews, save yourself."

38 There was a written notice above him, which read: THIS IS THE KING OF THE JEWS.

39 One of the criminals who hung there hurled insults at him: "Aren't you the Christ? Save yourself and us!"

40 But the other criminal rebuked him. "Don't you fear God," he said, "since you are under the same sentence? 41 We are punished justly, for we are getting what our deeds deserve. But this man has done nothing wrong."

42 Then he said, "Jesus, remember me when you come into your kingdom. c"

43 Jesus answered him, "I tell you the truth, today you will be with me in paradise."

Jesus' Death

44 It was now about the sixth hour, and darkness came over the whole land until the ninth hour, 45 for the sun stopped shining. And the curtain of the temple was torn

---

a 30 Hosea 10:8   b 34 Some early manuscripts do not have this sentence.   c 42 Some manuscripts come with your kingly power

---

23:34 *divided up his clothes.* Any possessions an executed person had with him were taken by the executioners. Unwittingly the soldiers (cf. Jn 19:23 – 24) were fulfilling the words of Ps 22:18.
23:43 *paradise.* In the Septuagint (the pre-Christian Greek translation of the OT) the word designated a garden (Ge 2:8 – 10) or forest (see Ne 2:8), but in the NT (used only here and in 2Co 12:4; Rev 2:7) it refers to the place of bliss and rest between death and resurrection (cf. Lk 16:22; 2Co 12:2).
23:45 *curtain of the temple.* The curtain between

in two. ⁴⁶Jesus called out with a loud voice, "Father, into your hands I commit my spirit." When he had said this, he breathed his last.

⁴⁷The centurion, seeing what had happened, praised God and said, "Surely this was a righteous man." ⁴⁸When all the people who had gathered to witness this

---

the Holy Place and the Most Holy Place. Its tearing symbolized Christ's opening the way directly to God (see Heb 9:3,8; 10:19–22).

23:47 *this was a righteous man.* Or "this man was the Righteous One." Matthew and Mark report the centurion's words as "this man was the Son (or

son) of God." "The Righteous One" and "the Son of God" would have been essentially equivalent terms. Similarly, "the son of God" and "a righteous man" would have been virtual equivalents. Which one the centurion intended is difficult to determine. It seems clear, however, that the

---

DID JESUS REALLY DIE ON THE CROSS?

THE CASE FOR
CHRIST
LUKE 23:46

CASE NO 42023046

Cynics who read the Gospels sometimes dispute the expertise of the Romans to determine whether Jesus was indeed dead. These soldiers were primitive in terms

> Jesus called out with a loud voice, "Father, into your hands I commit my spirit." When he had said this, he breathed his last.
>
> – LUKE 23:46

of their understanding of medicine and anatomy, so how do we know they weren't mistaken when they declared that Jesus was no longer living?

Though the soldiers didn't go to medical school, they were experts in killing people—that was their job, and they did it very well. They knew without a doubt when a person was dead, which is not difficult to figure out.

Besides, if a prisoner somehow escaped, the responsible soldiers would be put to death themselves, so they had a huge incentive to make absolutely sure that each and every victim was dead when he was removed from the cross.

—Adapted from interview with Dr. Alexander Metherell

sight saw what took place, they beat their breasts and went away. [49] But all those who knew him, including the women who had followed him from Galilee, stood at a distance, watching these things.

Jesus' Burial

[50] Now there was a man named Joseph, a member of the Council, a good and upright man, [51] who had not consented to their decision and action. He came from the Jude-

Gospel writers saw in his declaration a vindication of Jesus, and since the centurion was the Roman official in charge of the crucifixion, his testimony was viewed as significant (see also the declarations of Pilate: vv. 4,14–15,22; Mt 27:23–24).

WHY WOULD A MEMBER OF THE SANHEDRIN OFFER TO BURY JESUS?

Mark 14:64 states that the Sanhedrin "all condemned" Jesus to death. If that's true, wouldn't it mean that Joseph of Arimathea, a member of that body, cast his vote to kill Jesus? Isn't it highly unlikely that he would have offered his tomb for Jesus' burial?

"Luke may have felt this same discomfort," says apologist Dr. William Lane Craig, "which would explain why he added one important detail—Joseph of Arimathea wasn't present when the official vote was taken [see Luke 23:51]. That would explain the initial challenge. But the more significant point about Joseph of Arimathea is that he was not the sort of person who would have been invented by Christian legend or Christian authors.

"Given the early Christian anger and bitterness toward the Jewish leaders who had instigated the crucifixion of Jesus," he says, "it's highly improbable that they would have invented one who did the right thing by giving Jesus an honorable burial—especially while all of Jesus' disciples deserted him! Besides, they wouldn't make up a specific member of a specific group, whom

an town of Arimathea and he was waiting for the kingdom of God. ⁵²Going to Pilate, he asked for Jesus' body. ⁵³Then he took it down, wrapped it in linen cloth and placed it in a tomb cut in the rock, one in which no one had yet been laid. ⁵⁴It was Preparation Day, and the Sabbath was about to begin.

⁵⁵The women who had come with Jesus from Galilee followed Joseph and saw the tomb and how his body was laid in

---

23:52 The remains of an executed criminal often were left unburied or at best put in a dishonored place in a pauper's field. A near relative, such as a mother, might ask for the body, but it was a courageous gesture for Joseph, a member of the Sanhedrin, to ask for Jesus' body.

THE CASE FOR THE BIBLE

CASE NO. 42023050

LUKE 23:50–56

people could check out for themselves and ask about this. So Joseph is undoubtedly a historical figure.

"I'll add," says Craig, "that if this burial by Joseph were a legend that developed later, you'd expect to find other competing burial traditions about what happened to Jesus' body. However, you don't find these at all.

> Now there was a man named Joseph, a member of the Council, a good and upright man, who had not consented to their decision and action. He came from the Judean town of Arimathea and he was waiting for the kingdom of God. Going to Pilate, he asked for Jesus' body.
>
> — LUKE 23:50 - 52

"As a result, the majority of New Testament scholars today agree that the burial account of Jesus is fundamentally reliable. John A. T. Robinson, the late Cambridge University New Testament scholar, said the honorable burial of Jesus is one of the earliest and best-attested facts that we have about the historical Jesus."

—Adapted from interview with Dr. William Lane Craig

WAS JESUS' TOMB SECURE?

THE CASE FOR
CHRIST
LUKE 23:50–56

CASE NO 42023050

How secure was Jesus' grave? Archaeologists have been able to determine from excavations of first-century sites how Jesus' tomb was probably constructed.

> Going to Pilate, he asked for Jesus' body. Then he took it down, wrapped it in linen cloth and placed it in a tomb cut in the rock, one in which no one had yet been laid.
>
> — LUKE 23:52 - 53

There was likely a slanted groove that led down to a low entrance and a large disk-shaped stone was rolled down this groove and lodged into place across the door. A smaller stone was then used to secure the disk. Although it would be easy to roll this big disk down the groove, it would take several men to roll the stone back up in order to reopen the tomb. In short, it was quite secure.

In addition to the physical weight of the rock at the tomb's entrance, Matthew reports that guards stood watch around the tomb. In fact, Matthew adds the detail that when the guards reported Jesus' resurrection to the chief priests, the Jewish leaders paid them to say that they were sleeping while the disciples moved the large rock to steal the body (see Matthew 28:11–15 in the appendix at the back of this book). Of course, the disciples didn't have the motive, means or opportunity to actually take the body. Why would they do that and then knowingly and willingly die for what they knew was a lie? Actually, implicit in making up a cover story was the admission that Jesus' tomb really was empty on that first Easter morning.

—Adapted from interview with Dr. William Lane Craig

it. ⁵⁶Then they went home and prepared spices and perfumes. But they rested on the Sabbath in obedience to the commandment.

The Resurrection

24 On the first day of the week, very early in the morning, the women took the spices they had prepared and went to the tomb. ²They found the stone rolled away from the tomb, ³but when they entered, they did not find the body of the Lord Jesus. ⁴While they were wondering about this, suddenly two men in clothes that gleamed like lightning stood beside them. ⁵In their fright the women bowed down with their faces to the ground, but the men said to them, "Why do you look for the living among the dead? ⁶He is not here; he has risen! Remember how he told you, while he was still with you in Galilee: ⁷'The Son of Man must be delivered into the hands of sinful men, be crucified and on the third day be raised again.'" ⁸Then they remembered his words.

⁹When they came back from the tomb, they told all these things to the Eleven and to all the others. ¹⁰It was Mary Magdalene, Joanna, Mary the mother of James, and the others with them who told this to the apostles. ¹¹But they did not believe the women, because their words seemed to them like nonsense. ¹²Peter, however, got up and ran to the tomb. Bending over, he saw the strips of linen lying by themselves, and he went away, wondering to himself what had happened.

On the Road to Emmaus

¹³Now that same day two of them were going to a village called Emmaus, about seven miles^a from Jerusalem. ¹⁴They were talking with each other about everything that had happened. ¹⁵As they talked and discussed these things with each other, Jesus himself came up and walked along with them; ¹⁶but they were kept from recognizing him.

¹⁷He asked them, "What are you discussing together as you walk along?"

They stood still, their faces downcast. ¹⁸One of them, named Cleopas, asked him, "Are you only a visitor to Jerusalem and do not know the things that have happened there in these days?"

¹⁹"What things?" he asked.

"About Jesus of Nazareth," they replied. "He was a prophet, powerful in word and deed before God and all the people. ²⁰The chief priests and our rulers handed him over to be sentenced to death, and they crucified him; ²¹but we had hoped that he was the one who was going to redeem Israel. And what is more, it is the third day since all this took place. ²²In addition, some of our women amazed us. They went to the tomb early this morning ²³but didn't find his body. They came and told us that they had seen a vision of angels, who said he was alive. ²⁴Then some of our companions went to the tomb and found it just as the women had said, but him they did not see."

²⁵He said to them, "How foolish you are, and how slow of heart to believe all

---

^a 13 Greek *sixty stadia* (about 11 kilometers)

DO THE RESURRECTION ACCOUNTS IN THE FOUR GOSPELS CONTRADICT EACH OTHER?

A cursory reading of the resurrection accounts in Matthew, Mark, Luke and John reveals a few differences in the recorded facts. While these supposed discrepancies sometimes alarm modern readers, they tend not to concern historians because any differences are merely relegated to secondary details.

In each Gospel account the core story is the same: Joseph of Arimathea takes the body of Jesus and puts it in a tomb, one or more of Jesus' female followers visit the tomb early on the Sunday morning following his crucifixion, and they find that the tomb is empty. They see a vision of either one or two angels who say that Jesus is risen. Despite the differences concerning the women's number and names, the exact time of the morning and the number of angels, we can have great confidence in the shared core story that would be agreed upon by the majority of New Testament scholars today.

Even the usually skeptical historian Michael Grant, a fellow of Trinity College, Cambridge, and professor at Edinburgh University, concedes in his book *Jesus: An Historian's Review of the Gospels*: "True, the discovery of the empty tomb is differently described by the various gospels, but if we apply the same sort of criteria that we would apply to any other ancient literary sources, then the evidence is firm and plausible enough to necessitate the conclusion that the tomb was, indeed, found empty."

The differences between the empty tomb narratives are indicative of multiple, independent affirmations of the story. Sometimes people say, "Matthew and Luke just plagiarized from Mark," but when one examines the narratives closely, the divergences suggest that even if Matthew and Luke did know Mark's account, they also had separate, independent sources.

So with these multiple and independent accounts, no historian would disregard this evidence just because of secondary discrepancies. Consider the secular example of Hannibal crossing the Alps

CASE NO. 42024001

THE CASE FOR
CHRIST

LUKE 24:1-53

to attack Rome, for which there are two historically incompatible and irreconcilable accounts. Yet no classical historian doubts the fact that Hannibal did mount such a campaign. Hannibal's cross-

> When they came back from the tomb, they told all these things to the Eleven and to all the others. It was Mary Magdalene, Joanna, Mary the mother of James, and the others with them who told this to the apostles.
>
> — LUKE 24:9 - 10

ing is a nonbiblical illustration of a story in which discrepancies in secondary details fail to undermine the historical core accuracy of the event.

While that may be enough to satisfy historians, also consider that many of the alleged contradictions in the Gospel accounts are rather easily reconciled. For example, the accounts vary in the reported time of the visit to the tomb. One writer describes it as "still dark" (John 20:1), another says it was "very early in the morning" (Luke 24:1), and another says it was "just after sunrise" (Mark 16:2). But if the visit was "at dawn," (Matthew 28:1), they were likely describing the same thing with different words.

As for the number and names of the women, none of the Gospels pretends to give a complete list. They all include Mary Magdalene, and Matthew, Mark and Luke also cite other women, so there was probably a group of these early disciples that included those who were named and probably a couple of others. Perhaps when the women came, Mary Magdalene arrived first and that's why John mentions only her. That's hardly a contradiction.

In terms of whether there was one angel (Matthew) or two (John) at Jesus' tomb, have you ever noticed that whenever you have two of anything, you also have one? It never fails. Matthew didn't say there was *only* one. John was providing more detail by saying there were two.

—Adapted from interviews with Dr. William Lane Craig and Dr. Norman Geisler

WERE THE WOMEN
WITNESSES CREDIBLE?

The Gospels agree that women who were friends and followers of Jesus discovered the empty tomb. They also saw Jesus after his resurrection. To some, that makes their testimony suspect, since they were probably not objective observers. Does the women's relationship with Jesus call the reliability of their testimony into question?

"Actually, this argument backfires on people who use it," replies Dr. William Lane Craig, a research professor at Talbot School of Theology. "Certainly these women were friends of Jesus. But when you understand the role of women in first-century Jewish society, what's really extraordinary is that this empty tomb story should feature women as the discoverers of the empty tomb in the first place.

"Women were on a very low rung of the social ladder in first-century Palestine. There are old rabbinical sayings that said, 'Let the words of the Law be burned rather than delivered to women' and 'Blessed is he whose children are male, but woe to him whose children are female.' Women's testimony was regarded as so worthless that they weren't even allowed to serve as legal witnesses in a Jewish court of law.

"In light of this, it's absolutely remarkable that the chief witnesses to the empty tomb are these women who were friends of Jesus. Any later legendary account would have certainly portrayed male disciples as discovering the tomb—Peter or John, for example. The fact that women are the first witnesses to the empty tomb is most plausibly explained by the reality that—like it or not—they *were* the discoverers of the empty tomb! This shows that the Gospel writers faithfully recorded what happened, even if it was embarrassing. This bespeaks the historicity of this tradition rather than its legendary status."

THE CASE FOR
CHRIST
LUKE 24:1–12

CASE NO. 42024001

But do their actions make sense? Why were the women going to anoint the body of Jesus if they already knew that his tomb was securely sealed?

"These women were grieving, had lost someone they

> On the first day of the week, very early in the morning, the women took the spices they had prepared and went to the tomb. They found the stone rolled away from the tomb, but when they entered, they did not find the body of the Lord Jesus.
>
> — LUKE 24:1 – 3

desperately loved and followed, and wanted to go to the tomb in a forlorn hope of anointing the body," according to Craig. "Maybe they thought there would be men around who could move the stone. If there were guards, maybe they thought they would. I don't know. Certainly the notion of visiting a tomb to pour oils over a body is a historical Jewish practice; the only question is the feasibility of who would move the stone for them. And I don't think we're in the right position to pronounce judgment on whether or not they should have simply stayed at home."

—Adapted from interview with Dr. William Lane Craig

that the prophets have spoken! ²⁶Did not the Christ^a have to suffer these things and then enter his glory?" ²⁷And beginning with Moses and all the Prophets, he explained to them what was said in all the Scriptures concerning himself.

²⁸As they approached the village to which they were going, Jesus acted as if he were going farther. ²⁹But they urged him strongly, "Stay with us, for it is nearly evening; the day is almost over." So he went in to stay with them.

³⁰When he was at the table with them, he took bread, gave thanks, broke it and

^a 26 Or *Messiah*; also in verse 46

24:27 *Moses and all the Prophets.* A way of designating the whole of the OT Scriptures (see 16:16,29).

JESUS' APPEARANCE ON THE ROAD TO EMMAUS

Though some skeptics believe Jesus didn't actually die on the cross (but somehow survived the crucifixion), the story found in Luke 24:13–35—in which two disciples walked and talked with Jesus though "they were kept from recognizing him" (verse 16) by special divine intervention until the end of their time together—provides evidence of a genuine resurrection. Consider the alternative, that is, that Jesus somehow managed to survive the crucifixion, escape from his linen wrappings, roll the huge rock away from the mouth of his tomb, and get past the Roman soldiers who were standing guard. Medically speaking, he would have been in no condition to walk around after nails had been driven through his feet. He would not have been able to walk on the road to Emmaus, strolling for long distances. Remember, his arms had been stretched and pulled from their joints, he had massive wounds on his back and a spear wound to his side. A person in that kind of damaged condition would

began to give it to them. [31] Then their eyes were opened and they recognized him, and he disappeared from their sight. [32] They asked each other, "Were not our hearts burning within us while he talked with us on the road and opened the Scriptures to us?"

[33] They got up and returned at once to Jerusalem. There they found the Eleven and those with them, assembled together [34] and saying, "It is true! The Lord has risen and has appeared to Simon." [35] Then the two told what had happened on the way, and how Jesus was recognized by them when he broke the bread.

Jesus Appears to the Disciples

[36] While they were still talking about this, Jesus himself stood among them and said to them, "Peace be with you."

[37] They were startled and frightened, thinking they saw a ghost. [38] He said to

THE CASE FOR CHRIST

CASE NO. 42024013

LUKE 24:13–35

never have inspired his disciples to go out and proclaim him the Lord of life who had triumphed over the grave.

> Then their eyes were opened and they recognized him, and he disappeared from their sight.
>
> — LUKE 24:31

After suffering such horrible abuse, with all the catastrophic blood loss and trauma, Jesus would have looked so pitiful that the disciples would never have hailed him as a victorious conqueror of death; they would have felt sorry for him and tried to nurse him back to health. It's preposterous to think that if he had appeared to them in that awful state, his followers would have been prompted to start a worldwide movement based on the hope that someday they too would have a resurrection body like his.

—Adapted from interview with Dr. Alexander Metherell

WHO ENCOUNTERED THE RESURRECTED JESUS?

The risen Christ appeared to a lot of different people in the Gospels and Acts—some individually, some in groups, to softhearted people like John and to skeptical people like Thomas.

At times these people touched Jesus or ate with him, with the texts teaching that he was physically present. The appearances occurred over several weeks:

- Jesus appeared to Mary Magdalene (John 20:10–18);
- to the other women (Matthew 28:8–10; compare Matthew 28:1; Mark 16:1; Luke 24:10);
- to Cleopas and another disciple on the road to Emmaus (Luke 24:13–32);
- to Peter (Luke 24:34);
- to ten apostles and others, with Thomas absent (Luke 24:36–49; John 20:19–23);
- to Thomas and the other apostles (John 20:24–29);
- to seven apostles (John 21:1–14);
- to the eleven apostles (Matthew 28:16–20); and
- to the apostles at the Mount of Olives before his ascension (Luke 24:50–52; Acts 1:3–9).

C. H. Dodd, a Cambridge University scholar, has carefully analyzed these appearances and concluded that several of them are based on especially early material, including Jesus' encounter with the women, in Matthew 28:8–10; his meeting with the 11 apostles, when he gave them the Great Commission, in Matthew 28:16–20; and his meeting with the apostles, in John 20:24–29, when he showed them his hands and side.

Again, here was a wealth of sightings of Jesus. This was not merely a fleeting observance of a shadowy figure by one or two people. There were multiple appearances to numerous people, and several of the appearances were confirmed in more than one Gospel or by the creed in 1 Corinthians 15:3–7.

CASE NO. 42024036

THE CASE FOR
CHRIST
LUKE 24:36–49

In Acts, not only are Jesus' appearances mentioned regularly, but details are also provided, and the theme of the disciples being a witness of

> While they were still talking about this, Jesus himself stood among them and said to them, "Peace be with you."
>
> — LUKE 24:36

these things is found in almost every context. A number of the accounts in Acts 1–5, 10 and 13 also include some creeds that, like the one in 1 Corinthians 15, report some very early data concerning the death and resurrection of Jesus.

Indeed, Acts is littered with references to Jesus' appearances. The apostle Peter was especially adamant about it. He says in Acts 2:32, "God has raised this Jesus to life, and we are all witnesses of the fact." In Acts 3:15 he repeats, "You killed the author of life, but God raised him from the dead. We are witnesses of this." In Acts 10:41 he confirms to Cornelius and his family and friends that he and others "ate and drank with him after he rose from the dead."

Even Paul said in a speech recorded in Acts 13:30–31, "God raised him from the dead, and for many days he was seen by those who had traveled with him from Galilee to Jerusalem. They are now his witnesses to our people."

The resurrection was undoubtedly the central proclamation of the early church from the very beginning. The earliest Christians didn't just endorse Jesus' teachings; they were convinced they had seen him alive after his crucifixion. That's what changed their lives and started the church. Certainly, since this was their centermost conviction, they would have made absolutely sure that it was true.

All of the evidence from the Gospels and Acts—incident after incident, witness after witness, detail after detail, corroboration on top of corroboration—is extremely impressive. There may not be any more thoroughly attested event in ancient history.

—Adapted from interview with Dr. Gary Habermas

them, "Why are you troubled, and why do doubts rise in your minds? ³⁹ Look at my hands and my feet. It is I myself! Touch me and see; a ghost does not have flesh and bones, as you see I have."

⁴⁰ When he had said this, he showed them his hands and feet. ⁴¹ And while they still did not believe it because of joy and amazement, he asked them, "Do you have anything here to eat?" ⁴² They gave him a piece of broiled fish, ⁴³ and he took it and ate it in their presence.

⁴⁴ He said to them, "This is what I told you while I was still with you: Everything

WERE THE DISCIPLES SIMPLY HALLUCINATING OR VICTIMS OF GROUPTHINK?

Some people have suggested that the witnesses to Jesus' resurrection were sincere in believing they saw him but that they were actually experiencing a hallucination that convinced them they were encountering Jesus when they really weren't.

The first problem with this theory is that hallucinations can't be shared, and there are repeated accounts of Jesus appearing to multiple people who reported the same thing. Additionally, there are several other arguments why hallucinations can't explain away his appearances.

The disciples were fearful, doubtful and in despair after the crucifixion, whereas people who hallucinate need a fertile, open mind. Also, hallucinations are rare, usually caused by drugs or bodily deprivation. (Chances are you don't know anybody who's ever had a hallucination not caused by one of those two things.)

It's certainly unlikely that over a course of many weeks, people from all sorts of backgrounds, all kinds of temperaments and in various places all experienced similar hallucinations. And what about the empty tomb? If people only thought they saw Jesus, his body would still be in his grave.

Could this have been an example of groupthink, in which people talk each other into seeing something that doesn't ex-

must be fulfilled that is written about me in the Law of Moses, the Prophets and the Psalms."

⁴⁵ Then he opened their minds so they could understand the Scriptures. ⁴⁶ He told them, "This is what is written: The

24:44 *Law of Moses, the Prophets and the Psalms.* The three parts of the Hebrew OT (Psalms was the most prominent book of the third section, called the Writings), indicating that Christ (the Messiah) was foretold in the whole OT.

THE CASE FOR CHRIST
LUKE 24:37–49

CASE NO 42024037

ist? This doesn't seem plausible because the resurrection was the center of their faith, and there was too much at stake for them to needlessly go to their deaths defending it. Wouldn't some of them later rethink the groupthink and recant or just quietly fall away?

They were startled and frightened, thinking they saw a ghost. He said to them, "Why are you troubled, and why do doubts rise in your minds? Look at my hands and my feet. It is I myself! Touch me and see; a ghost does not have flesh and bones, as you see I have."

— LUKE 24:37-39

And what about Jesus' half brother James, who didn't believe in Jesus, and Paul, who was trying to destroy Christianity—how did they get talked into seeing the resurrected Jesus? They were not predisposed to imagining his presence if he wasn't really there. And again, what about the empty tomb? This view doesn't account for the clear language of the creed in 1 Corinthians 15:3–7 and other passages.

Sometimes people just grasp at straws trying to account for the resurrection appearances. But nothing fits all the evidence better than the explanation that Jesus was alive.

—Adapted from interview with Dr. Gary Habermas

Christ will suffer and rise from the dead on the third day, ⁴⁷ and repentance and forgiveness of sins will be preached in his name to all nations, beginning at Jerusalem. ⁴⁸ You are witnesses of these things. ⁴⁹ I am going to send you what my Father has promised; but stay in the city until you have been clothed with power from on high."

The Ascension

⁵⁰ When he had led them out to the vicinity of Bethany, he lifted up his hands and blessed them. ⁵¹ While he was blessing them, he left them and was taken up into heaven. ⁵² Then they worshiped him and returned to Jerusalem with great joy. ⁵³ And they stayed continually at the temple, praising God.

24:46 *suffer ... rise from the dead ... third day.* See 1Co 15:3–4. The OT depicts the Messiah as one who would suffer (see Isa 53) and rise from the dead on the third day (compare Ps 16:8–11 with Ac 2:23–33; see Isa 53:10–11; compare Jnh 1:17 with Mt 12:40).
24:47 *repentance and forgiveness of sins.* See Ac 5:31; 10:43; 13:38; 26:18. The prediction of

Christ's death and resurrection (v. 46) is joined with the necessary human response (repentance) and the resulting benefit (forgiveness; cf. Isa 49:6; Ac 13:47; 26:22–23).
24:49 *what my Father has promised.* See Joel 2:28–32. The reference is to the coming power of the Spirit, fulfilled in Ac 2:4 (see also Ac 2:17–22).

PART

THREE

MINIMAL FACTS THAT MAKE THE CASE FOR THE RESURRECTION

It was a rare opportunity: there I was, sitting across from *Playboy* founder Hugh Hefner in his opulent Los Angeles mansion, discussing spiritual issues for a television show I was hosting.

Clad in his trademark pajamas and silk smoking jacket, Hefner professed a minimal belief in God. But the God of Christianity, he said, was "a little too childlike for me."

Interestingly, when I brought up Jesus' resurrection, Hefner immediately recognized its significance. "If one had any real evidence that, indeed, Jesus did return from the dead, then that is the beginning of a dropping of a series of dominoes that takes us to all kinds of wonderful things," he told me. "It assures an afterlife and all kinds of things that we would all hope are true."

But even though he had never looked into the historical evidence for Jesus returning to life, Hefner remained a doubter. "I don't think that [Jesus] is any more the Son of God than we are," he said.

Hefner was right about one thing: everything hinges on the resurrection. If it's true, it confirms Jesus' identity as the unique Son of God and opens the door for eternal life to his followers. If it's a legend or mistake, then Jesus is just another unfortunate crucifixion victim in a long line of revolutionaries and false messiahs.

Nearly 20 centuries ago, the physician Luke, a companion of the apostle Paul, who himself encountered the resurrected Jesus, went to original sources to produce his own account of Jesus' physical return from the dead. Other independent and early accounts are contained in the Gospels of Matthew and John, who were both disciples, and the Gospel of Mark, who conveys the eyewitness account of the disciple Peter. The resurrection is repeatedly confirmed elsewhere in the New Testament, especially the books Acts and 1 Corinthians.

In recent years, however, a new approach to documenting the evidence for the resurrection has been pioneered by renowned resurrection historian Dr. Gary Habermas. To hear first-hand about this unique analysis, I invited Habermas' colleague and coauthor, Dr. Michael Licona, over to my house to discuss it.

As a prominent defender of the historicity resurrection, Licona has debated atheist Richard Carrier, Muslim Shabir Ally, agnostic Bart Ehrman and other skeptics. His dissertation toward his doctorate in New Testament from the University of

Pretoria in South Africa used historical methodologies to assess the evidence for Jesus returning from the dead.

In 2004, he joined Habermas in writing *The Case for the Resurrection of Jesus,* an award-winning book that historian Paul Maier called "the most comprehensive treatment of the subject anywhere."[1] It was in this book that Habermas and Licona detailed the "minimal facts approach" to Jesus' resurrection.

Getting past prejudices

"You can't deny that you see the historical evidence through the lenses of your own prejudices," I said to Licona as we sat in my family room.

"Absolutely. Nobody is exempt, including theists, deists, atheists or whatever — we all have our biases and there's no way to overcome them," Licona said. "That's why you have to put certain checks and balances in place. This is what Habermas did in creating what's called the 'minimal facts approach' to the resurrection."

"How does this keep biases in check?"

"Under this approach, we only consider facts that meet two criteria. First, there must be very strong historical evidence supporting them. And, secondly, the evidence must be so strong that the vast majority of today's scholars on the subject — *including skeptical ones* — accept these as historical facts."

"History isn't a vote," I interjected. "Are you saying people should accept these facts just because a lot of scholars do?"

"No, we're saying that this evidence is so good that even skeptical scholars are con-vinced by it. Let's face it: there's a greater likelihood that a purported historical fact is true when someone accepts it even though they're not in agreement with your metaphysical beliefs."

"How do you know what these scholars believe?" I asked.

"Habermas has compiled a list of more than 2,200 sources in French, German and English in which experts have written on the resurrection from 1975 to the present," Licona said. "He has identified minimal facts that are strongly evidenced and which are regarded as historical by the large majority of scholars, including skeptics. We try to come up with the best historical explanation to account for these facts."

With that background in place, I invited Licona to build the case for Jesus rising from the dead. "I'll use just five minimal facts," he said, "and you can decide for yourself how persuasive the case is."

FACT #1:

Jesus was killed by crucifixion

According to Licona, "Even an extreme liberal like [John Dominic] Crossan says: 'That he was crucified is as sure as any-thing historical ever can be.'[2] Skeptic James Tabor says, 'I think we need have no doubt that given Jesus' execution by Roman crucifixion he was truly *dead.*'[3] Both Gerd Lüdemann, who's an atheistic New Testament critic, and Bart Ehrman, who's an agnostic, call the crucifixion an indisputable fact.

"Why? First of all, because all four Gos-pels report it. We also have a number of non-Christian sources that corroborate the crucifixion. For instance, the historian Tacitus said Jesus 'suffered the extreme penalty during the reign of Tiberius.' The Jewish historian Josephus reports that Pilate 'condemned him to be crucified.' Lucian of Samosata, who was a Greek satirist, mentions the crucifixion, and Mara Bar-Serapion, who was a pagan, confirms Jesus was executed. Even the Jewish Talmud reports that [Jesus was killed].

"Jesus was crucified and died as a result. The scholarly consensus — again, even among those who are skeptical toward the resurrection — is absolutely overwhelming. To deny it would be to take a marginal position that would get you laughed out of the academic world."

FACT #2
Jesus' disciples believed that he rose and appeared to them

"The second fact is the disciples' beliefs that Jesus had actually returned from the dead and had appeared to them," Licona said. "There are three strands of evidence for this: Paul's testimony about the disciples; oral traditions that passed through the early church; and the written works of the early church.

"Paul is important because he reports knowing some of the disciples personally, including Peter, James and John. Acts confirms this.[4] And Paul says in 1 Corinthians 15:11 that whether 'it was I or they, this is what we preach,' referring to the resurrection of Jesus. So in other words, Paul knew the apostles and reports that they

claimed — just as he did — that Jesus had returned from the dead.

"Then we have oral tradition. Obviously, people in those days didn't have tape recorders and few people could read, so they relied on verbal transmission for passing along what happened until it was later written down. Scholars have identified several places in which this oral tradition has been copied into the New Testament in the form of creeds, hymns and sermon summations. This is really significant because the oral tradition must have existed prior to the New Testament writings for the New Testament authors to have included them."

"So it's early," I said.

"Very early, which weighs heavily in their favor. For example, we have creeds that laid out basic doctrines in a form that was easily memorized. One of the earliest and most important creeds was relayed by Paul in his first letter to the Corinthian church, which was written about A.D. 55. It says:

> For what I received I passed on to you as of first importance: that Christ died for our sins according to the Scriptures, that he was buried, that he was raised on the third day according to the Scriptures, and that he appeared to Peter, and then to the Twelve. After that, he appeared to more than five hundred of the brothers at the same time, most of whom are still living, though some have fallen asleep. Then he appeared to James, then to all the apostles ...[5]

"Many scholars believe Paul received this creed from Peter and James while visiting with them in Jerusalem three years after his conversion. That would be within five years of the crucifixion. Not only is it extremely early, but it was apparently given to Paul by eyewitnesses or others he deemed reliable, which heightens its credibility even more."

"How important is this creed?"

"It's powerful and persuasive," he declared. "Although early dating does not totally rule out the possibility of invention or deceit on the part of Jesus' followers, it is much too early to be the result of legendary development over time, since it can practically be traced to the original disciples of Jesus. In fact, this creed has been one of the most formidable obstacles to critics who try to shoot down the resurrection.

"And we've got even more oral tradition — for instance, the New Testament preserves several sermons of the apostles. Actually, these are apparently summaries of the preaching. At a minimum, we can say that the vast majority of historians believe that the early apostolic teachings are enshrined in these sermon summaries in Acts — and they declare that Jesus rose bodily from the dead.

"For example, Paul says in Acts 13, which is very similar to what Peter reports in Acts 2: 'For when David had served God's purpose in his own generation, he fell asleep; he was buried with his fathers and his body decayed. But the one whom God raised from the dead did not see decay.'[6] That's a bold assertion: David's body decayed, but Jesus' didn't, because he was raised from the dead.

"Finally we have written sources, such as Matthew, Mark, Luke and John. It's widely accepted, even among skeptical historians, that the Gospels were written in the first century. Even very liberal scholars will concede that we have four biographies written within 70 years of Jesus' life that unambiguously report the disciples' claims that Jesus rose from the dead.

"I think an excellent case can be made for dating the Gospels earlier, but let's go with the more generous estimations. That's still extremely close to the events themselves, especially compared to many other ancient historical writings. Our two best sources on Alexander the Great, for instance, weren't written until at least 400 years after his life.

"Then we have the writings of the apostolic fathers, who were said to have known the apostles or were close to others who did. There's a strong likelihood that their writings reflect the teachings of the apostles themselves — and what do they say? That the apostles were dramatically impacted by Jesus' resurrection.

"Consider Clement, for example. The early church father Irenaeus reports that Clement had conversed with the apostles. Tertullian, the African church father, said Clement was ordained by Peter himself."

"So what does Clement report about the disciples?" I asked.

"In his letter to the Corinthian church, written in the first century, he writes: 'Therefore, having received ... complete certainty caused by the resurrection of our Lord Jesus Christ ... they went ... preaching the good news that the kingdom of God is about to come.'[7]

"Then we have Polycarp. Irenaeus says

that Polycarp was 'instructed by the apostles, and conversed with many who had seen Christ,' including John. Tertullian confirms that John appointed Polycarp as bishop of the church in Smyrna. Around A.D. 110, Polycarp wrote a letter to the Philippian church in which he mentions the resurrection of Jesus no fewer than five times.

"So think about the depth of evidence we have in these three categories: Paul, oral tradition and written reports. In all, we've got nine sources that reflect multiple, very early and eyewitness testimonies to the disciples' claims that they had seen the risen Jesus. This is something the disciples believed to the core of their being."

"How do you know that?"

"Because we have evidence that the disciples had been transformed to the point where they were willing to endure persecution and even martyrdom. Just read through Acts and you'll see how the disciples were willing to suffer for their conviction that Jesus rose from the dead. The church fathers Clement, Polycarp, Ignatius, Tertullian and Origen — they all confirm this. In fact, we've got at least seven early sources testifying that the disciples willingly suffered in defense of their beliefs — and if we include the martyrdoms of Paul and Jesus' half-brother James, we have eleven sources."

"But," I objected, "people of other faiths have been willing to die for their beliefs through the ages — so what does the martyrdom of the disciples really prove?"

"First, it means that they certainly regarded their beliefs to be true," he said.

"They didn't willfully lie about this. Liars make poor martyrs. Second, the disciples didn't just *believe* Jesus rose from the dead, but they knew for a fact whether or not he did. They were on the scene and able to ascertain for sure that he had been resurrected. So it was for the *truth* of the resurrection that they were willing to die.

"This is totally different than a modern-day Islamic terrorist or others willing to die for their beliefs. These people can only have faith that their beliefs are true, but they aren't in a position to know for sure. The disciples, on the other hand, knew for a *fact* whether the resurrection had truly occurred — and knowing the *truth*, they were willing to die for the belief that they had."

"Then what's the bottom line?" I asked.

"Habermas completed an overview of more than two thousand scholarly sources on the resurrection going back 30 years — and probably no fact was more widely recognized than that the early Christian believers had real experiences that they thought were appearances of the risen Jesus," Licona replied.

"Even the atheist Lüdemann conceded: 'It may be taken as historically certain that Peter and the disciples had experiences after Jesus' death in which Jesus appeared to them as the risen Christ.'[8] Now, he claims this was the result of visions, which I simply don't believe is a credible explanation. But he's conceding that their experiences actually occurred."

Licona also cited liberal scholar Paula Fredriksen of Boston University, who said, "The disciples' conviction that they had seen the risen Christ ... is [part of] historical bedrock, facts known past doubting."[9]

"I think that's pretty much undeniable," said Licona. "And I believe the evidence is clear and convincing that what they saw was the return of Jesus from the dead."

FACT #3

The conversion of the church persecutor Paul

"We know from multiple sources that Paul — then known as Saul of Tarsus — was an enemy of the church and committed to persecuting the faithful," Licona said. "But Paul himself says that he was converted to a follower of Jesus because he had personally encountered the resurrected Jesus.[10] So we have Jesus' resurrection attested to by friend and foe alike, which is very significant.

"Then we have six ancient sources in addition to Paul — such as Luke, Clement of Rome, Polycarp, Tertullian, Dionysius of Corinth and Origen — reporting that Paul was willing to suffer continuously and even die for his beliefs. Again, liars make poor martyrs. So we can be confident that Paul not only claimed the risen Jesus appeared to him, but that he really believed it.

"You can't claim that Paul was a friend of Jesus who was primed to see a vision of him due to wishful thinking or grief after his crucifixion. His mindset was to oppose the Christian movement that he believed was following a false messiah. His radical transformation from persecutor to missionary demands an explanation — and I think the best explanation is that he's telling the truth when he says he met the risen Jesus.

"He had nothing to gain in this world — except his own suffering and martyrdom — for making this up."

FACT #4:

The conversion of the skeptic James, Jesus' half-brother

"The next minimal fact involves James, the half-brother of Jesus," Licona said. "We have good evidence that James was not a follower of Jesus during Jesus' lifetime. Mark and John both report that none of Jesus' brothers believed in him."[11]

These reports are most likely true, he said, because "people are not going to invent a story that's going to be embarrassing or potentially discrediting to them, and it would be particularly humiliating for a first-century rabbi not to have his own family as his followers.

"Then, however, the pivotal moment occurs: the ancient creedal material in 1 Corinthians 15 tells us that the risen Jesus appeared to James. Again, this is an extremely early account that has all the earmarks of reliability. In fact, James may have been involved in passing along this creed to Paul, in which case James would be personally endorsing what the creed reports about him.

"As a result of his encounter with the risen Jesus, James didn't just become a Christian, but he later became leader of the Jerusalem church.[12] Actually, James was so thoroughly convinced of Jesus' messiahship because of the resurrection that he died as a martyr, as both Christian and non-Christian sources attest.[13]

"So here we have another example of a skeptic who was converted because of a personal encounter with the resurrected Lord and was willing to die for his convictions."

FACT #5

Jesus' tomb was empty

"Although the fifth fact — that the tomb of Jesus was empty — is part of the minimal case for the resurrection, it doesn't enjoy the nearly universal consensus among scholars that the first four do," explained Licona.

"Still, there's strong evidence in its favor. Habermas determined that about 75 percent of scholars on the subject regard it as a historical fact. Personally, I think the empty tomb is very well-supported if the historical data are assessed without preconceptions. Basically, there are three strands of evidence: the Jerusalem factor, enemy attestation and the testimony of women."

"Jerusalem factor?" I asked.

"This refers to the fact that Jesus was publicly executed and buried in Jerusalem and then his resurrection was proclaimed in the very same city. In fact, several weeks after the crucifixion, Peter declared to a crowd in Jerusalem: 'God has raised this Jesus to life, and we are all witnesses of the fact.'[14] Frankly, it would have been impossible for Christianity to get off the ground in Jerusalem if Jesus' body were still in the tomb. The Roman or Jewish authorities could have simply gone over to his tomb, viewed his corpse, and the misunderstanding would have been over.

"Instead, what we do hear is enemy attestation to the empty tomb. In other words, what were the skeptics saying? That the disciples stole the body. This is reported not only by Matthew, but also by Justin Martyr and Tertullian. Here's the thing: Why would you say someone stole the body if it were still in the tomb? This is an implicit admission that the tomb was empty.

"On top of that, the idea that the disciples stole the body is a lame explanation. Are we supposed to believe they conspired to steal the body, pulled it off, and then were willing to suffer continuously and even die for what they knew was a lie? That's such an absurd idea that scholars universally reject it today. In addition, we have the testimony of women that the tomb was empty."

"Why is this important?" I asked.

"Because in both first-century Jewish and Roman cultures, women were lowly esteemed and their testimony was considered very questionable," Licona explained. "If you were going to concoct a story in an effort to fool others, you would never in that day have hurt your own credibility by saying that women discovered the empty tomb. It would be extremely unlikely that the Gospel writers would invent testimony like this, because they wouldn't get any mileage out of it. In fact, it could hurt them. If they had felt the freedom simply to make things up, surely they'd claim that men — maybe Peter or John — were the first to find the tomb empty.

"The best theory for why the Gospel writers would include such an embarrassing detail is because that's what actually happened and they were committed to recording it accurately, regardless of the credibility problem it created.

"So when you consider the Jerusalem factor, the enemy attestation and the testimony of women, there are good historical reasons for concluding Jesus' tomb was empty. William Ward of Oxford University put it this way: 'All the strictly historical evidence we have is in favor [of the empty tomb], and those scholars who reject it ought to recognize that they do so on some other ground than that of scientific history.'"[15]

"Okay, how would you summarize your case?" I asked.

"Shortly after Jesus died from crucifixion, his disciples believed that they saw him risen from the dead. They said he appeared not only to individuals but in several group settings — and the disciples were so convinced and transformed by the experience that they were willing to suffer and even die for their conviction that they had encountered him.

"Then we have two skeptics who regarded Jesus as a false prophet — Paul, the persecutor of the church, and James, who was Jesus' half-brother. They completely changed their opinions 180 degrees after encountering the risen Jesus. Like the disciples, they were willing to endure hardship, persecution and even death rather than disavow their testimony that Jesus' resurrection occurred.

"Thus we have compelling testimony about the resurrection from friends of Jesus, an enemy of Christianity and a skeptic. Finally, we have strong historical evidence that Jesus' tomb was empty. In fact, even enemies of Christianity admitted it was vacant. Where did the body go? If you asked the disciples, they'd tell you they personally saw Jesus after he returned to life.

"What's the best explanation for the evidence — the explanation that doesn't leave out any of the facts or doesn't strain to make anything fit? My conclusion, based on the evidence, is that Jesus did return from the dead. No other explanation comes close to accounting for all of the facts. Historically speaking, I think we've got a cogent and convincing case."

Licona could have presented all kinds of historical evidence for the resurrection, but instead he limited himself only to five facts that are extremely well-attested and that the vast majority of scholars — including skeptics — concede are trustworthy.

I had to agree: the case was cogent and compelling. As historian N. T. Wright, author of *The Resurrection of the Son of God*, put it:

It is no good falling back on "science" as having disproved the possibility of resurrection. Any real scientist will tell you that science observes what normally happens; the Christian case is precisely that what happened to Jesus is not what normally happens. For my part, as a historian I prefer the elegant, essentially simple solution rather than the one that fails to include all the data: to say that the early Christians believed that Jesus had been bodily raised from the dead, and to account for this belief by saying that they were telling the truth.[16]

Notes

1. Gary R. Habermas and Michael R. Licona, *The Case for the Resurrection of Jesus* (Grand Rapids, MI: Kregel, 2004), 1.

2. John Dominic Crossan, *Jesus: a Revolutionary Biography* (San Francisco: HarperCollins, 1991), 145.

3. James D. Tabor, *The Jesus Dynasty* (New York: Simon & Schuster, 2006), 230 (emphasis in original).

4. See: Acts 9:26–30; 15:1–35.

5. 1 Corinthians 15:3–7.

6. See: Acts 13:36–37.

7. First Clement 42:3.

8. Gerd Lüdemann, *What Really Happened to Jesus?* (John Bowden, translator) (Louisville: Westminster John Knox, 1995), 80.

9. Paula Fredriksen, *Jesus of Nazareth* (New York: Vintage, 1999), 264.

10. See: 1 Corinthians 9:1 and 15:8; Acts 9, 22, and 26.

11. See: Mark 3:21; 6:3–4; and John 7:3–5.

12. See: Acts 15:12–21 and Galatians 1:19.

13. See: Josephus (*Ant.* 20:200); Hegesippus (quoted by Eusebius in *EH* 2:23); Clement of Alexandria (quoted by Eusebius in *EH* 2:1, 23.)

14. Acts 2:32.

15. William Ward, *Christianity: A Historical Religion?* (Valley Forge, PA.: Judson, 1972), 93–94.

16. Marcus Borg and N. T. Wright, *The Meaning of Jesus: Two Visions* (San Francisco: HarperSanFrancisco, 1999), 124–125.

PART

FOUR

My original investigation of Christianity, which began when I first read Luke's Gospel while I was still an atheist, consumed a year and nine months of my life, culminating on a Sunday afternoon as I spent some time alone in my bedroom.

After accumulating so much evidence, I knew it was time to reach a verdict. So I took a yellow legal pad and began summarizing all of the historical data I had encountered during my 21-month odyssey.

I filled page after page after page after page — until finally I realized that in light of the avalanche of evidence that points so powerfully toward the truth of Christianity, it would have required more faith to maintain my atheism than to become a Christian. Seriously! Maintaining my atheism would have been like swimming upstream against a torrent of facts flowing the other direction. I couldn't do that. I had been trained in journalism and law to respond to truth.

At that moment, I reached my verdict: based on the historical data, I was convinced that Jesus not only claimed to be the Son of God, but he also validated that claim by returning from the dead.

I put down my pen. *Was that it? Was I finished? Is that all there is?* I felt like I was stuck. But then I remembered a verse that a Christian friend had pointed out to me once. I dug out my Bible and quickly found John 1:12: "Yet to all who received him, to those who believed in his name, he gave the right to become children of God."

This verse forms an equation of what it means to become a child of God: Believe + Receive = Become. I realized at that moment that to *believe* Jesus is the unique Son of God is an important step, but it's simply not enough. I had to personally *receive* his free gift of forgiveness and eternal life that he purchased for me when he died on the cross as my substitute to pay for all of my wrongdoing — past, present and future. Only then would I *become* a child of God.

That's when I sank to my knees next to my bed and poured out a confession of a lifetime of immorality. At that moment, I received complete and total forgiveness through Christ — and that's when I became a child of God forever.

There were no lightning bolts, no audible replies from God himself, no tingly sensations. I know that some people feel a rush of emotion at such a moment; as for me, however, there was something else that was equally exhilarating: *there was the rush of reason.*

"I will remove your heart of stone"

My very next thought was that maybe Leslie would like to know what I've done. So I emerged from our bedroom, walked down the hallway and looked into the kitchen, where I saw Leslie behind the kitchen sink. Our daughter Alison, who by then was nearly five years old, was standing in front of her. Alison was on her toes and reaching out to touch the faucet. It was the first time she had been able to reach it.

"Look, daddy — I can reach it!" she exclaimed. "I can touch it!"

"That's great," I said as I gave her a big hug and she scampered off.

I turned to Leslie. "You know, that's exactly how I feel," I told her. "I've been reaching for someone for a long time, and today I was finally able to touch him. Jesus is resurrected, he's alive, and I just gave him my life."

Leslie burst into tears and threw her arms around my neck. "Oh, honey, I didn't know what to do," she said between sobs. "When I was a new Christian, I met some women at church and I told them, 'I don't have any hope for my husband. He's the hardheaded, hard-hearted legal editor of *The Chicago Tribune*. He'll never bend his knee to Jesus Christ.'"

Then Leslie described for me how one woman had put her arm around her shoulder and told her, "Oh, Leslie, no one is beyond hope." And the woman showed her a verse from the Old Testament, Ezekiel 36:26, which says, "I will give you a new heart and put a new spirit in you; I will remove from you your heart of stone and give you a heart of flesh."

Unbeknownst to me, Leslie had prayed that verse for me during the entire two years of my spiritual quest. Starting on that Sunday afternoon — not overnight,

but over time as I opened my life more and more to God — God began to answer that prayer.

Soon my character began to change. And so did my values. And so did my morality and my attitude and my philosophy and my worldview and my relationships and my priorities. Over time, my whole life began to change — for the good.

So radical was the difference that even my young daughter took notice. Think about it: all Alison had known in the early years of her life was a daddy who was absent and angry, profane and drunken, verbally harsh and narcissistic. But she started to watch from her little five-year-old perspective as her father began to walk God's path. She never interviewed a scholar, never analyzed the historical record, never studied archaeology, but she could clearly see the positive influence God was having on her dad.

Finally, one day she came first to her Sunday school teacher and then to Leslie and said, "I want God to do for me what he's done for daddy."

In effect, she was saying, *If this is the kind of positive change that God creates in people — then sign me up!* So at age five, Alison became a follower of Jesus. Today, she's a vibrant Christian, the author of a series of Christian novels, the wife of a seminary graduate who writes Christian books for children, the mother of my two precious granddaughters — and she and I are the closest of friends.

The same thing is true of my son, Kyle. He also became a follower of Jesus, received his undergraduate degree in

Biblical studies, earned master's degrees in philosophy of religion and New Testament, and is completing his doctorate in theology at the University of Aberdeen in Scotland. His life's mission: to help people experience Jesus as a way of life.

God changed me, he changed my wife, he changed my son, and he changed my daughter. And that's my story.

So what about you?

Reaching your own verdict

Let's go back to that formula for faith: Believe + Receive = Become. If you don't yet believe, then let me encourage you to do what I did: conduct your own thorough investigation of the evidence.

You might want to take advantage of *The Case for Christ Study Bible* and examine its study notes and in-depth articles, which put the totality of Scripture into context and trace the case for the Messiah from the Old Testament to the New Testament.

I urge you to keep an open mind, make this a front-burner issue in your life and resolve to reach your own verdict when the evidence is in. As the Bible promises in Jeremiah 29:13: "You will seek me and find me when you seek me with all your heart."

But perhaps you already believe that Jesus established his divine credentials by returning from the dead. You may not have answers to every single one of your peripheral questions, but keep in mind that you don't have to know *everything* to know *something*. You can know with confidence that Jesus claimed to be the Son of God and then backed up that claim by rising from his tomb. *That's enough for now.*

All that remains for you to become a child of God is to receive Jesus as your forgiver and leader — your Lord and Savior — in a prayer of repentance and faith. In fact, you could tell Jesus essentially the same thing I told him on November 8, 1981:

Lord Jesus, it's true that I've fallen short of how you want me to live. In fact, I've sinned in more ways than I can count, and I'm truly sorry for that. I want to turn from my path and begin to walk yours. As best I can, I believe that you are the unique Son of God who died for my sins and was resurrected back to life. Right now I reach out to receive your free gift of forgiveness and eternal life. Thank you for going to the cross to pay the penalty for all of my wrongdoing so that I can be reconciled with God and become his child. Please lead my life. Help me to live as you want me to live — because from this moment on, I am yours.

APPENDIX

MATTHEW'S ACCOUNT OF THE DEATH AND RESURRECTION OF JESUS

Matthew 26:1–75; 27:1–66; 28:1–20

The Plot Against Jesus

26 When Jesus had finished saying all these things, he said to his disciples, [2]"As you know, the Passover is two days away — and the Son of Man will be handed over to be crucified."

[3]Then the chief priests and the elders of the people assembled in the palace of the high priest, whose name was Caiaphas, [4]and they plotted to arrest Jesus in some sly way and kill him. [5]"But not during the Feast," they said, "or there may be a riot among the people."

Jesus Anointed at Bethany

[6]While Jesus was in Bethany in the home of a man known as Simon the Leper, [7]a woman came to him with an alabaster jar of very expensive perfume, which she poured on his head as he was reclining at the table.

[8]When the disciples saw this, they were indignant. "Why this waste?" they asked. [9]"This perfume could have been sold at a high price and the money given to the poor."

[10]Aware of this, Jesus said to them, "Why are you bothering this woman? She has done a beautiful thing to me. [11]The poor you will always have with you, but you will not always have me. [12]When she poured this perfume on my body, she did it to prepare me for burial. [13]I tell you the truth, wherever this gospel is preached throughout the world, what she has done will also be told, in memory of her."

Judas Agrees to Betray Jesus

[14]Then one of the Twelve — the one called Judas Iscariot — went to the chief priests [15]and asked, "What are you willing to give me if I hand him over to you?" So they counted out for him thirty silver coins. [16]From then on Judas watched for an opportunity to hand him over.

The Lord's Supper

[17]On the first day of the Feast of Unleavened Bread, the disciples came to Jesus and asked, "Where do you want us to make preparations for you to eat the Passover?"

[18]He replied, "Go into the city to a certain man and tell him, 'The Teacher says: My appointed time is near. I am going to celebrate the Passover with my disciples at your house.'" [19]So the disciples did as

Jesus had directed them and prepared the Passover.

20 When evening came, Jesus was reclining at the table with the Twelve. 21 And while they were eating, he said, "I tell you the truth, one of you will betray me."

22 They were very sad and began to say to him one after the other, "Surely not I, Lord?"

23 Jesus replied, "The one who has dipped his hand into the bowl with me will betray me. 24 The Son of Man will go just as it is written about him. But woe to that man who betrays the Son of Man! It would be better for him if he had not been born."

25 Then Judas, the one who would betray him, said, "Surely not I, Rabbi?"

Jesus answered, "Yes, it is you."a

26 While they were eating, Jesus took bread, gave thanks and broke it, and gave it to his disciples, saying, "Take and eat; this is my body."

27 Then he took the cup, gave thanks and offered it to them, saying, "Drink from it, all of you. 28 This is my blood of theb covenant, which is poured out for many for the forgiveness of sins. 29 I tell you, I will not drink of this fruit of the vine from now on until that day when I drink it anew with you in my Father's kingdom."

30 When they had sung a hymn, they went out to the Mount of Olives.

Jesus Predicts Peter's Denial

31 Then Jesus told them, "This very night you will all fall away on account of me, for it is written:

"'I will strike the shepherd,
    and the sheep of the flock will be
        scattered.'c

32 But after I have risen, I will go ahead of you into Galilee."

33 Peter replied, "Even if all fall away on account of you, I never will."

34 "I tell you the truth," Jesus answered, "this very night, before the rooster crows, you will disown me three times."

35 But Peter declared, "Even if I have to die with you, I will never disown you." And all the other disciples said the same.

Gethsemane

36 Then Jesus went with his disciples to a place called Gethsemane, and he said to them, "Sit here while I go over there and pray." 37 He took Peter and the two sons of Zebedee along with him, and he began to be sorrowful and troubled. 38 Then he said to them, "My soul is overwhelmed with sorrow to the point of death. Stay here and keep watch with me."

39 Going a little farther, he fell with his face to the ground and prayed, "My Father, if it is possible, may this cup be taken from me. Yet not as I will, but as you will."

40 Then he returned to his disciples and found them sleeping. "Could you men not keep watch with me for one hour?" he asked Peter. 41 "Watch and pray so that you will not fall into temptation. The spirit is willing, but the body is weak."

42 He went away a second time and prayed, "My Father, if it is not possible for

a 25 Or "You yourself have said it"   b 28 Some manuscripts the new   c 31 Zech. 13:7

this cup to be taken away unless I drink it, may your will be done."

⁴³When he came back, he again found them sleeping, because their eyes were heavy. ⁴⁴So he left them and went away once more and prayed the third time, saying the same thing.

⁴⁵Then he returned to the disciples and said to them, "Are you still sleeping and resting? Look, the hour is near, and the Son of Man is betrayed into the hands of sinners. ⁴⁶Rise, let us go! Here comes my betrayer!"

Jesus Arrested

⁴⁷While he was still speaking, Judas, one of the Twelve, arrived. With him was a large crowd armed with swords and clubs, sent from the chief priests and the elders of the people. ⁴⁸Now the betrayer had arranged a signal with them: "The one I kiss is the man; arrest him." ⁴⁹Going at once to Jesus, Judas said, "Greetings, Rabbi!" and kissed him.

⁵⁰Jesus replied, "Friend, do what you came for."ᵃ

Then the men stepped forward, seized Jesus and arrested him. ⁵¹With that, one of Jesus' companions reached for his sword, drew it out and struck the servant of the high priest, cutting off his ear.

⁵²"Put your sword back in its place," Jesus said to him, "for all who draw the sword will die by the sword. ⁵³Do you think I cannot call on my Father, and he will at once put at my disposal more than twelve legions of angels? ⁵⁴But how then would the Scriptures be fulfilled that say it must happen in this way?"

⁵⁵At that time Jesus said to the crowd, "Am I leading a rebellion, that you have come out with swords and clubs to capture me? Every day I sat in the temple courts teaching, and you did not arrest me. ⁵⁶But this has all taken place that the writings of the prophets might be fulfilled." Then all the disciples deserted him and fled.

Before the Sanhedrin

⁵⁷Those who had arrested Jesus took him to Caiaphas, the high priest, where the teachers of the law and the elders had assembled. ⁵⁸But Peter followed him at a distance, right up to the courtyard of the high priest. He entered and sat down with the guards to see the outcome.

⁵⁹The chief priests and the whole Sanhedrin were looking for false evidence against Jesus so that they could put him to death. ⁶⁰But they did not find any, though many false witnesses came forward.

Finally two came forward ⁶¹and declared, "This fellow said, 'I am able to destroy the temple of God and rebuild it in three days.'"

⁶²Then the high priest stood up and said to Jesus, "Are you not going to answer? What is this testimony that these men are bringing against you?" ⁶³But Jesus remained silent.

The high priest said to him, "I charge you under oath by the living God: Tell us if you are the Christ,ᵇ the Son of God."

⁶⁴"Yes, it is as you say," Jesus replied. "But I say to all of you: In the future you will see the Son of Man sitting at the right

ᵃ 50 Or "Friend, why have you come?"   ᵇ 63 Or Messiah; also in verse 68 hand of the Mighty One and coming on the clouds of heaven."

65 Then the high priest tore his clothes and said, "He has spoken blasphemy! Why do we need any more witnesses? Look, now you have heard the blasphemy. 66 What do you think?"

"He is worthy of death," they answered.

67 Then they spit in his face and struck him with their fists. Others slapped him 68 and said, "Prophesy to us, Christ. Who hit you?"

Peter Disowns Jesus

69 Now Peter was sitting out in the courtyard, and a servant girl came to him. "You also were with Jesus of Galilee," she said.

70 But he denied it before them all. "I don't know what you're talking about," he said.

71 Then he went out to the gateway, where another girl saw him and said to the people there, "This fellow was with Jesus of Nazareth."

72 He denied it again, with an oath: "I don't know the man!"

73 After a little while, those standing there went up to Peter and said, "Surely you are one of them, for your accent gives you away."

74 Then he began to call down curses on himself and he swore to them, "I don't know the man!"

Immediately a rooster crowed. 75 Then Peter remembered the word Jesus had spoken: "Before the rooster crows, you will disown me three times." And he went outside and wept bitterly.

Judas Hangs Himself

27 Early in the morning, all the chief priests and the elders of the people came to the decision to put Jesus to death. 2 They bound him, led him away and handed him over to Pilate, the governor.

3 When Judas, who had betrayed him, saw that Jesus was condemned, he was seized with remorse and returned the thirty silver coins to the chief priests and the elders. 4 "I have sinned," he said, "for I have betrayed innocent blood."

"What is that to us?" they replied. "That's your responsibility."

5 So Judas threw the money into the temple and left. Then he went away and hanged himself.

6 The chief priests picked up the coins and said, "It is against the law to put this into the treasury, since it is blood money." 7 So they decided to use the money to buy the potter's field as a burial place for foreigners. 8 That is why it has been called the Field of Blood to this day. 9 Then what was spoken by Jeremiah the prophet was fulfilled: "They took the thirty silver coins, the price set on him by the people of Israel, 10 and they used them to buy the potter's field, as the Lord commanded me."[a]

Jesus Before Pilate

11 Meanwhile Jesus stood before the governor, and the governor asked him, "Are you the king of the Jews?"

"Yes, it is as you say," Jesus replied.

12 When he was accused by the chief priests and the elders, he gave no answer.

a 10 See Zech. 11:12,13; Jer. 19:1-13; 32:6-9.

[13] Then Pilate asked him, "Don't you hear the testimony they are bringing against you?" [14] But Jesus made no reply, not even to a single charge — to the great amazement of the governor.

[15] Now it was the governor's custom at the Feast to release a prisoner chosen by the crowd. [16] At that time they had a notorious prisoner, called Barabbas. [17] So when the crowd had gathered, Pilate asked them, "Which one do you want me to release to you: Barabbas, or Jesus who is called Christ?" [18] For he knew it was out of envy that they had handed Jesus over to him.

[19] While Pilate was sitting on the judge's seat, his wife sent him this message: "Don't have anything to do with that innocent man, for I have suffered a great deal today in a dream because of him."

[20] But the chief priests and the elders persuaded the crowd to ask for Barabbas and to have Jesus executed.

[21] "Which of the two do you want me to release to you?" asked the governor.

"Barabbas," they answered.

[22] "What shall I do, then, with Jesus who is called Christ?" Pilate asked.

They all answered, "Crucify him!"

[23] "Why? What crime has he committed?" asked Pilate.

But they shouted all the louder, "Crucify him!"

[24] When Pilate saw that he was getting nowhere, but that instead an uproar was starting, he took water and washed his hands in front of the crowd. "I am innocent of this man's blood," he said. "It is your responsibility!"

[25] All the people answered, "Let his blood be on us and on our children!"

[26] Then he released Barabbas to them. But he had Jesus flogged, and handed him over to be crucified.

The Soldiers Mock Jesus

[27] Then the governor's soldiers took Jesus into the Praetorium and gathered the whole company of soldiers around him. [28] They stripped him and put a scarlet robe on him, [29] and then twisted together a crown of thorns and set it on his head. They put a staff in his right hand and knelt in front of him and mocked him. "Hail, king of the Jews!" they said. [30] They spit on him, and took the staff and struck him on the head again and again. [31] After they had mocked him, they took off the robe and put his own clothes on him. Then they led him away to crucify him.

The Crucifixion

[32] As they were going out, they met a man from Cyrene, named Simon, and they forced him to carry the cross. [33] They came to a place called Golgotha (which means The Place of the Skull). [34] There they offered Jesus wine to drink, mixed with gall; but after tasting it, he refused to drink it. [35] When they had crucified him, they divided up his clothes by casting lots.[a] [36] And sitting down, they kept watch over him there. [37] Above his head they placed the written charge against him: THIS IS

[a] 35 A few late manuscripts *lots that the word spoken by the prophet might be fulfilled: "They divided my garments among themselves and cast lots for my clothing"* (Psalm 22:18)

JESUS, THE KING OF THE JEWS. [38] Two robbers were crucified with him, one on his right and one on his left. [39] Those who passed by hurled insults at him, shaking their heads [40] and saying, "You who are going to destroy the temple and build it in three days, save yourself! Come down from the cross, if you are the Son of God!"

[41] In the same way the chief priests, the teachers of the law and the elders mocked him. [42] "He saved others," they said, "but he can't save himself! He's the King of Israel! Let him come down now from the cross, and we will believe in him. [43] He trusts in God. Let God rescue him now if he wants him, for he said, 'I am the Son of God.'" [44] In the same way the robbers who were crucified with him also heaped insults on him.

The Death of Jesus

[45] From the sixth hour until the ninth hour darkness came over all the land. [46] About the ninth hour Jesus cried out in a loud voice, *"Eloi, Eloi,[a] lama sabachthani?"* — which means, "My God, my God, why have you forsaken me?"[b]

[47] When some of those standing there heard this, they said, "He's calling Elijah."

[48] Immediately one of them ran and got a sponge. He filled it with wine vinegar, put it on a stick, and offered it to Jesus to drink. [49] The rest said, "Now leave him alone. Let's see if Elijah comes to save him."

[50] And when Jesus had cried out again in a loud voice, he gave up his spirit.

[51] At that moment the curtain of the temple was torn in two from top to bottom. The earth shook and the rocks split. [52] The tombs broke open and the bodies of many holy people who had died were raised to life. [53] They came out of the tombs, and after Jesus' resurrection they went into the holy city and appeared to many people.

[54] When the centurion and those with him who were guarding Jesus saw the earthquake and all that had happened, they were terrified, and exclaimed, "Surely he was the Son[c] of God!"

[55] Many women were there, watching from a distance. They had followed Jesus from Galilee to care for his needs. [56] Among them were Mary Magdalene, Mary the mother of James and Joses, and the mother of Zebedee's sons.

The Burial of Jesus

[57] As evening approached, there came a rich man from Arimathea, named Joseph, who had himself become a disciple of Jesus. [58] Going to Pilate, he asked for Jesus' body, and Pilate ordered that it be given to him. [59] Joseph took the body, wrapped it in a clean linen cloth, [60] and placed it in his own new tomb that he had cut out of the rock. He rolled a big stone in front of the entrance to the tomb and went away. [61] Mary Magdalene and the other Mary were sitting there opposite the tomb.

The Guard at the Tomb

[62] The next day, the one after Preparation Day, the chief priests and the Pharisees went to Pilate. [63] "Sir," they said, "we remember that while he was still alive that

---

[a] 46 Some manuscripts *Eli, Eli*   [b] 46 Psalm 22:1   [c] 54 Or *a son*

deceiver said, 'After three days I will rise again.' [64] So give the order for the tomb to be made secure until the third day. Otherwise, his disciples may come and steal the body and tell the people that he has been raised from the dead. This last deception will be worse than the first."

[65] "Take a guard," Pilate answered. "Go, make the tomb as secure as you know how." [66] So they went and made the tomb secure by putting a seal on the stone and posting the guard.

The Resurrection

28 After the Sabbath, at dawn on the first day of the week, Mary Magdalene and the other Mary went to look at the tomb.

[2] There was a violent earthquake, for an angel of the Lord came down from heaven and, going to the tomb, rolled back the stone and sat on it. [3] His appearance was like lightning, and his clothes were white as snow. [4] The guards were so afraid of him that they shook and became like dead men.

[5] The angel said to the women, "Do not be afraid, for I know that you are looking for Jesus, who was crucified. [6] He is not here; he has risen, just as he said. Come and see the place where he lay. [7] Then go quickly and tell his disciples: 'He has risen from the dead and is going ahead of you into Galilee. There you will see him.' Now I have told you."

[8] So the women hurried away from the tomb, afraid yet filled with joy, and ran to tell his disciples. [9] Suddenly Jesus met them. "Greetings," he said. They came to him, clasped his feet and worshiped him. [10] Then Jesus said to them, "Do not be afraid. Go and tell my brothers to go to Galilee; there they will see me."

The Guards' Report

[11] While the women were on their way, some of the guards went into the city and reported to the chief priests everything that had happened. [12] When the chief priests had met with the elders and devised a plan, they gave the soldiers a large sum of money, [13] telling them, "You are to say, 'His disciples came during the night and stole him away while we were asleep.' [14] If this report gets to the governor, we will satisfy him and keep you out of trouble." [15] So the soldiers took the money and did as they were instructed. And this story has been widely circulated among the Jews to this very day.

The Great Commission

[16] Then the eleven disciples went to Galilee, to the mountain where Jesus had told them to go. [17] When they saw him, they worshiped him; but some doubted. [18] Then Jesus came to them and said, "All authority in heaven and on earth has been given to me. [19] Therefore go and make disciples of all nations, baptizing them in[a] the name of the Father and of the Son and of the Holy Spirit, [20] and teaching them to obey everything I have commanded you. And surely I am with you always, to the very end of the age."

[a] 19 Or into; see Acts 8:16; 19:5; Romans 6:3; 1 Cor. 1:13; 10:2 and Gal. 3:27.

MARK'S ACCOUNT OF THE DEATH AND RESURRECTION OF JESUS

Mark 14:1–72; 15:1–47; 16:1–20

Jesus Anointed at Bethany

14 Now the Passover and the Feast of Unleavened Bread were only two days away, and the chief priests and the teachers of the law were looking for some sly way to arrest Jesus and kill him. [2] "But not during the Feast," they said, "or the people may riot."

[3] While he was in Bethany, reclining at the table in the home of a man known as Simon the Leper, a woman came with an alabaster jar of very expensive perfume, made of pure nard. She broke the jar and poured the perfume on his head.

[4] Some of those present were saying indignantly to one another, "Why this waste of perfume? [5] It could have been sold for more than a year's wages[a] and the money given to the poor." And they rebuked her harshly.

[6] "Leave her alone," said Jesus. "Why are you bothering her? She has done a beautiful thing to me. [7] The poor you will always have with you, and you can help them any time you want. But you will not always have me. [8] She did what she could. She poured perfume on my body beforehand to prepare for my burial. [9] I tell you the truth, wherever the gospel is preached throughout the world, what she has done will also be told, in memory of her."

[10] Then Judas Iscariot, one of the Twelve, went to the chief priests to betray Jesus to them. [11] They were delighted to hear this and promised to give him money. So he watched for an opportunity to hand him over.

The Lord's Supper

[12] On the first day of the Feast of Unleavened Bread, when it was customary to sacrifice the Passover lamb, Jesus' disciples asked him, "Where do you want us to go and make preparations for you to eat the Passover?"

[13] So he sent two of his disciples, telling them, "Go into the city, and a man carrying a jar of water will meet you. Follow him. [14] Say to the owner of the house he enters, 'The Teacher asks: Where is my guest room, where I may eat the Passover with my disciples?' [15] He will show you a large

---

[a] 5 Greek *than three hundred denarii*

upper room, furnished and ready. Make preparations for us there."

¹⁶ The disciples left, went into the city and found things just as Jesus had told them. So they prepared the Passover.

¹⁷ When evening came, Jesus arrived with the Twelve. ¹⁸ While they were reclining at the table eating, he said, "I tell you the truth, one of you will betray me — one who is eating with me."

¹⁹ They were saddened, and one by one they said to him, "Surely not I?"

²⁰ "It is one of the Twelve," he replied, "one who dips bread into the bowl with me. ²¹ The Son of Man will go just as it is written about him. But woe to that man who betrays the Son of Man! It would be better for him if he had not been born."

²² While they were eating, Jesus took bread, gave thanks and broke it, and gave it to his disciples, saying, "Take it; this is my body."

²³ Then he took the cup, gave thanks and offered it to them, and they all drank from it.

²⁴ "This is my blood of the*a* covenant, which is poured out for many," he said to them. ²⁵ "I tell you the truth, I will not drink again of the fruit of the vine until that day when I drink it anew in the kingdom of God."

²⁶ When they had sung a hymn, they went out to the Mount of Olives.

Jesus Predicts Peter's Denial

²⁷ "You will all fall away," Jesus told them, "for it is written:

" 'I will strike the shepherd,
   and the sheep will be scattered.'*b*

²⁸ But after I have risen, I will go ahead of you into Galilee."

²⁹ Peter declared, "Even if all fall away, I will not."

³⁰ "I tell you the truth," Jesus answered, "today — yes, tonight — before the rooster crows twice*c* you yourself will disown me three times."

³¹ But Peter insisted emphatically, "Even if I have to die with you, I will never disown you." And all the others said the same.

Gethsemane

³² They went to a place called Gethsemane, and Jesus said to his disciples, "Sit here while I pray." ³³ He took Peter, James and John along with him, and he began to be deeply distressed and troubled. ³⁴ "My soul is overwhelmed with sorrow to the point of death," he said to them. "Stay here and keep watch."

³⁵ Going a little farther, he fell to the ground and prayed that if possible the hour might pass from him. ³⁶ "Abba,*d* Father," he said, "everything is possible for you. Take this cup from me. Yet not what I will, but what you will."

³⁷ Then he returned to his disciples and found them sleeping. "Simon," he said to Peter, "are you asleep? Could you not keep watch for one hour? ³⁸ Watch and pray so that you will not fall into temptation. The spirit is willing, but the body is weak."

³⁹ Once more he went away and prayed

---

a 24 Some manuscripts *the new*   *b 27* Zech. 13:7   *c 30* Some early manuscripts do not have *twice.*
d 36 Aramaic for *Father*

the same thing. [40] When he came back, he again found them sleeping, because their eyes were heavy. They did not know what to say to him.

[41] Returning the third time, he said to them, "Are you still sleeping and resting? Enough! The hour has come. Look, the Son of Man is betrayed into the hands of sinners. [42] Rise! Let us go! Here comes my betrayer!"

Jesus Arrested

[43] Just as he was speaking, Judas, one of the Twelve, appeared. With him was a crowd armed with swords and clubs, sent from the chief priests, the teachers of the law, and the elders.

[44] Now the betrayer had arranged a signal with them: "The one I kiss is the man; arrest him and lead him away under guard." [45] Going at once to Jesus, Judas said, "Rabbi!" and kissed him. [46] The men seized Jesus and arrested him. [47] Then one of those standing near drew his sword and struck the servant of the high priest, cutting off his ear.

[48] "Am I leading a rebellion," said Jesus, "that you have come out with swords and clubs to capture me? [49] Every day I was with you, teaching in the temple courts, and you did not arrest me. But the Scriptures must be fulfilled." [50] Then everyone deserted him and fled.

[51] A young man, wearing nothing but a linen garment, was following Jesus. When they seized him, [52] he fled naked, leaving his garment behind.

Before the Sanhedrin

[53] They took Jesus to the high priest, and all the chief priests, elders and teachers of the law came together. [54] Peter followed him at a distance, right into the courtyard of the high priest. There he sat with the guards and warmed himself at the fire.

[55] The chief priests and the whole Sanhedrin were looking for evidence against Jesus so that they could put him to death, but they did not find any. [56] Many testified falsely against him, but their statements did not agree.

[57] Then some stood up and gave this false testimony against him: [58] "We heard him say, 'I will destroy this man-made temple and in three days will build another, not made by man.' " [59] Yet even then their testimony did not agree.

[60] Then the high priest stood up before them and asked Jesus, "Are you not going to answer? What is this testimony that these men are bringing against you?" [61] But Jesus remained silent and gave no answer.

Again the high priest asked him, "Are you the Christ,[a] the Son of the Blessed One?"

[62] "I am," said Jesus. "And you will see the Son of Man sitting at the right hand of the Mighty One and coming on the clouds of heaven."

[63] The high priest tore his clothes. "Why do we need any more witnesses?" he asked. [64] "You have heard the blasphemy. What do you think?"

They all condemned him as worthy of death. [65] Then some began to spit at him;

[a] 61 Or *Messiah*

they blindfolded him, struck him with their fists, and said, "Prophesy!" And the guards took him and beat him.

Peter Disowns Jesus

⁶⁶While Peter was below in the courtyard, one of the servant girls of the high priest came by. ⁶⁷When she saw Peter warming himself, she looked closely at him.

"You also were with that Nazarene, Jesus," she said.

⁶⁸But he denied it. "I don't know or understand what you're talking about," he said, and went out into the entryway.ᵃ

⁶⁹When the servant girl saw him there, she said again to those standing around, "This fellow is one of them." ⁷⁰Again he denied it.

After a little while, those standing near said to Peter, "Surely you are one of them, for you are a Galilean."

⁷¹He began to call down curses on himself, and he swore to them, "I don't know this man you're talking about."

⁷²Immediately the rooster crowed the second time.ᵇ Then Peter remembered the word Jesus had spoken to him: "Before the rooster crows twiceᶜ you will disown me three times." And he broke down and wept.

Jesus Before Pilate

15 Very early in the morning, the chief priests, with the elders, the teachers of the law and the whole Sanhedrin, reached a decision. They bound Jesus, led him away and handed him over to Pilate.

²"Are you the king of the Jews?" asked Pilate.

"Yes, it is as you say," Jesus replied.

³The chief priests accused him of many things. ⁴So again Pilate asked him, "Aren't you going to answer? See how many things they are accusing you of."

⁵But Jesus still made no reply, and Pilate was amazed.

⁶Now it was the custom at the Feast to release a prisoner whom the people requested. ⁷A man called Barabbas was in prison with the insurrectionists who had committed murder in the uprising. ⁸The crowd came up and asked Pilate to do for them what he usually did.

⁹"Do you want me to release to you the king of the Jews?" asked Pilate, ¹⁰knowing it was out of envy that the chief priests had handed Jesus over to him. ¹¹But the chief priests stirred up the crowd to have Pilate release Barabbas instead.

¹²"What shall I do, then, with the one you call the king of the Jews?" Pilate asked them.

¹³"Crucify him!" they shouted.

¹⁴"Why? What crime has he committed?" asked Pilate.

But they shouted all the louder, "Crucify him!"

¹⁵Wanting to satisfy the crowd, Pilate released Barabbas to them. He had Jesus flogged, and handed him over to be crucified.

ᵃ 68 Some early manuscripts *entryway and the rooster crowed*   ᵇ 72 Some early manuscripts do not have *the second time.*   ᶜ 72 Some early manuscripts do not have *twice.*

The Soldiers Mock Jesus

¹⁶The soldiers led Jesus away into the palace (that is, the Praetorium) and called together the whole company of soldiers. ¹⁷They put a purple robe on him, then twisted together a crown of thorns and set it on him. ¹⁸And they began to call out to him, "Hail, king of the Jews!" ¹⁹Again and again they struck him on the head with a staff and spit on him. Falling on their knees, they paid homage to him. ²⁰And when they had mocked him, they took off the purple robe and put his own clothes on him. Then they led him out to crucify him.

The Crucifixion

²¹A certain man from Cyrene, Simon, the father of Alexander and Rufus, was passing by on his way in from the country, and they forced him to carry the cross. ²²They brought Jesus to the place called Golgotha (which means The Place of the Skull). ²³Then they offered him wine mixed with myrrh, but he did not take it. ²⁴And they crucified him. Dividing up his clothes, they cast lots to see what each would get.

²⁵It was the third hour when they crucified him. ²⁶The written notice of the charge against him read: THE KING OF THE JEWS. ²⁷They crucified two robbers with him, one on his right and one on his left.^a ²⁹Those who passed by hurled insults at him, shaking their heads and saying, "So! You who are going to destroy the temple and build it in three days, ³⁰come down from the cross and save yourself!"

³¹In the same way the chief priests and the teachers of the law mocked him among themselves. "He saved others," they said, "but he can't save himself! ³²Let this Christ,^b this King of Israel, come down now from the cross, that we may see and believe." Those crucified with him also heaped insults on him.

The Death of Jesus

³³At the sixth hour darkness came over the whole land until the ninth hour. ³⁴And at the ninth hour Jesus cried out in a loud voice, *"Eloi, Eloi, lama sabachthani?"* — which means, "My God, my God, why have you forsaken me?"^c

³⁵When some of those standing near heard this, they said, "Listen, he's calling Elijah."

³⁶One man ran, filled a sponge with wine vinegar, put it on a stick, and offered it to Jesus to drink. "Now leave him alone. Let's see if Elijah comes to take him down," he said.

³⁷With a loud cry, Jesus breathed his last.

³⁸The curtain of the temple was torn in two from top to bottom. ³⁹And when the centurion, who stood there in front of Jesus, heard his cry and^d saw how he died, he said, "Surely this man was the Son^e of God!"

⁴⁰Some women were watching from a distance. Among them were Mary Magdalene, Mary the mother of James the

---

^a 27 Some manuscripts *left, ²⁸and the scripture was fulfilled which says, "He was counted with the lawless ones"* (Isaiah 53:12)   ^b 32 Or *Messiah*   ^c 34 Psalm 22:1   ^d 39 Some manuscripts do not have *heard his cry and*   ^e 39 Or *a son*

younger and of Joses, and Salome. [41]In Galilee these women had followed him and cared for his needs. Many other women who had come up with him to Jerusalem were also there.

The Burial of Jesus

[42]It was Preparation Day (that is, the day before the Sabbath). So as evening approached, [43]Joseph of Arimathea, a prominent member of the Council, who was himself waiting for the kingdom of God, went boldly to Pilate and asked for Jesus' body. [44]Pilate was surprised to hear that he was already dead. Summoning the centurion, he asked him if Jesus had already died. [45]When he learned from the centurion that it was so, he gave the body to Joseph. [46]So Joseph bought some linen cloth, took down the body, wrapped it in the linen, and placed it in a tomb cut out of rock. Then he rolled a stone against the entrance of the tomb. [47]Mary Magdalene and Mary the mother of Joses saw where he was laid.

The Resurrection

16 When the Sabbath was over, Mary Magdalene, Mary the mother of James, and Salome bought spices so that they might go to anoint Jesus' body. [2]Very early on the first day of the week, just after sunrise, they were on their way to the tomb [3]and they asked each other, "Who will roll the stone away from the entrance of the tomb?"

[4]But when they looked up, they saw that the stone, which was very large, had been rolled away. [5]As they entered the tomb, they saw a young man dressed in a white robe sitting on the right side, and they were alarmed.

[6]"Don't be alarmed," he said. "You are looking for Jesus the Nazarene, who was crucified. He has risen! He is not here. See the place where they laid him. [7]But go, tell his disciples and Peter, 'He is going ahead of you into Galilee. There you will see him, just as he told you.'"

[8]Trembling and bewildered, the women went out and fled from the tomb. They said nothing to anyone, because they were afraid.

[The earliest manuscripts and some other ancient witnesses do not have Mark 16:9 – 20.]

[9]When Jesus rose early on the first day of the week, he appeared first to Mary Magdalene, out of whom he had driven seven demons. [10]She went and told those who had been with him and who were mourning and weeping. [11]When they heard that Jesus was alive and that she had seen him, they did not believe it.

[12]Afterward Jesus appeared in a different form to two of them while they were walking in the country. [13]These returned and reported it to the rest; but they did not believe them either.

[14]Later Jesus appeared to the Eleven as they were eating; he rebuked them for their lack of faith and their stubborn refusal to believe those who had seen him after he had risen.

[15]He said to them, "Go into all the world and preach the good news to all creation.

¹⁶Whoever believes and is baptized will be saved, but whoever does not believe will be condemned. ¹⁷And these signs will accompany those who believe: In my name they will drive out demons; they will speak in new tongues; ¹⁸they will pick up snakes with their hands; and when they drink deadly poison, it will not hurt them at all; they will place their hands on sick people, and they will get well."

¹⁹After the Lord Jesus had spoken to them, he was taken up into heaven and he sat at the right hand of God. ²⁰Then the disciples went out and preached everywhere, and the Lord worked with them and confirmed his word by the signs that accompanied it.

JOHN'S ACCOUNT OF THE DEATH AND RESURRECTION OF JESUS

John 12:1–11; 18:1–40; 19:1–42; 20:1–31; 21:1–25

Jesus Anointed at Bethany

12 Six days before the Passover, Jesus arrived at Bethany, where Lazarus lived, whom Jesus had raised from the dead. ²Here a dinner was given in Jesus' honor. Martha served, while Lazarus was among those reclining at the table with him. ³Then Mary took about a pint*a* of pure nard, an expensive perfume; she poured it on Jesus' feet and wiped his feet with her hair. And the house was filled with the fragrance of the perfume.

⁴But one of his disciples, Judas Iscariot, who was later to betray him, objected, ⁵"Why wasn't this perfume sold and the money given to the poor? It was worth a year's wages.*b*" ⁶He did not say this because he cared about the poor but because he was a thief; as keeper of the money bag, he used to help himself to what was put into it.

⁷"Leave her alone," Jesus replied. " ⌐ It was intended ⌐ that she should save this perfume for the day of my burial. ⁸You will always have the poor among you, but you will not always have me."

⁹Meanwhile a large crowd of Jews found out that Jesus was there and came, not only because of him but also to see Lazarus, whom he had raised from the dead. ¹⁰So the chief priests made plans to kill Lazarus as well, ¹¹for on account of him many of the Jews were going over to Jesus and putting their faith in him.

Jesus Arrested

18 When he had finished praying, Jesus left with his disciples and crossed the Kidron Valley. On the other side there was an olive grove, and he and his disciples went into it.

²Now Judas, who betrayed him, knew the place, because Jesus had often met there with his disciples. ³So Judas came to the grove, guiding a detachment of soldiers and some officials from the chief priests and Pharisees. They were carrying torches, lanterns and weapons.

⁴Jesus, knowing all that was going to happen to him, went out and asked them, "Who is it you want?"

⁵"Jesus of Nazareth," they replied.

"I am he," Jesus said. (And Judas the traitor was standing there with them.)

---

a 3 Greek *a litra* (probably about 0.5 liter) *b* 5 Greek *three hundred denarii*

⁶When Jesus said, "I am he," they drew back and fell to the ground.

⁷Again he asked them, "Who is it you want?"

And they said, "Jesus of Nazareth."

⁸"I told you that I am he," Jesus answered. "If you are looking for me, then let these men go." ⁹This happened so that the words he had spoken would be fulfilled: "I have not lost one of those you gave me."ᵃ

¹⁰Then Simon Peter, who had a sword, drew it and struck the high priest's servant, cutting off his right ear. (The servant's name was Malchus.)

¹¹Jesus commanded Peter, "Put your sword away! Shall I not drink the cup the Father has given me?"

Jesus Taken to Annas

¹²Then the detachment of soldiers with its commander and the Jewish officials arrested Jesus. They bound him ¹³and brought him first to Annas, who was the father-in-law of Caiaphas, the high priest that year. ¹⁴Caiaphas was the one who had advised the Jews that it would be good if one man died for the people.

Peter's First Denial

¹⁵Simon Peter and another disciple were following Jesus. Because this disciple was known to the high priest, he went with Jesus into the high priest's courtyard, ¹⁶but Peter had to wait outside at the door. The other disciple, who was known to the high priest, came back, spoke to the girl on duty there and brought Peter in.

¹⁷"You are not one of his disciples, are you?" the girl at the door asked Peter.

He replied, "I am not."

¹⁸It was cold, and the servants and officials stood around a fire they had made to keep warm. Peter also was standing with them, warming himself.

The High Priest Questions Jesus

¹⁹Meanwhile, the high priest questioned Jesus about his disciples and his teaching.

²⁰"I have spoken openly to the world," Jesus replied. "I always taught in synagogues or at the temple, where all the Jews come together. I said nothing in secret. ²¹Why question me? Ask those who heard me. Surely they know what I said."

²²When Jesus said this, one of the officials nearby struck him in the face. "Is this the way you answer the high priest?" he demanded.

²³"If I said something wrong," Jesus replied, "testify as to what is wrong. But if I spoke the truth, why did you strike me?" ²⁴Then Annas sent him, still bound, to Caiaphas the high priest.ᵇ

Peter's Second and Third Denials

²⁵As Simon Peter stood warming himself, he was asked, "You are not one of his disciples, are you?"

He denied it, saying, "I am not."

²⁶One of the high priest's servants, a relative of the man whose ear Peter had cut

ᵃ 9 John 6:39   ᵇ 24 Or (Now Annas had sent him, still bound, to Caiaphas the high priest.)

off, challenged him, "Didn't I see you with him in the olive grove?" ²⁷Again Peter denied it, and at that moment a rooster began to crow.

Jesus Before Pilate

²⁸Then the Jews led Jesus from Caiaphas to the palace of the Roman governor. By now it was early morning, and to avoid ceremonial uncleanness the Jews did not enter the palace; they wanted to be able to eat the Passover. ²⁹So Pilate came out to them and asked, "What charges are you bringing against this man?"

³⁰"If he were not a criminal," they replied, "we would not have handed him over to you."

³¹Pilate said, "Take him yourselves and judge him by your own law."

"But we have no right to execute anyone," the Jews objected. ³²This happened so that the words Jesus had spoken indicating the kind of death he was going to die would be fulfilled.

³³Pilate then went back inside the palace, summoned Jesus and asked him, "Are you the king of the Jews?"

³⁴"Is that your own idea," Jesus asked, "or did others talk to you about me?"

³⁵"Am I a Jew?" Pilate replied. "It was your people and your chief priests who handed you over to me. What is it you have done?"

³⁶Jesus said, "My kingdom is not of this world. If it were, my servants would fight to prevent my arrest by the Jews. But now my kingdom is from another place."

³⁷"You are a king, then!" said Pilate.

Jesus answered, "You are right in saying I am a king. In fact, for this reason I was born, and for this I came into the world, to testify to the truth. Everyone on the side of truth listens to me."

³⁸"What is truth?" Pilate asked. With this he went out again to the Jews and said, "I find no basis for a charge against him. ³⁹But it is your custom for me to release to you one prisoner at the time of the Passover. Do you want me to release 'the king of the Jews'?"

⁴⁰They shouted back, "No, not him! Give us Barabbas!" Now Barabbas had taken part in a rebellion.

Jesus Sentenced to Be Crucified

19 Then Pilate took Jesus and had him flogged. ²The soldiers twisted together a crown of thorns and put it on his head. They clothed him in a purple robe ³and went up to him again and again, saying, "Hail, king of the Jews!" And they struck him in the face.

⁴Once more Pilate came out and said to the Jews, "Look, I am bringing him out to you to let you know that I find no basis for a charge against him." ⁵When Jesus came out wearing the crown of thorns and the purple robe, Pilate said to them, "Here is the man!"

⁶As soon as the chief priests and their officials saw him, they shouted, "Crucify! Crucify!"

But Pilate answered, "You take him and crucify him. As for me, I find no basis for a charge against him."

⁷The Jews insisted, "We have a law, and according to that law he must die, because he claimed to be the Son of God."

[8] When Pilate heard this, he was even more afraid, [9] and he went back inside the palace. "Where do you come from?" he asked Jesus, but Jesus gave him no answer. [10] "Do you refuse to speak to me?" Pilate said. "Don't you realize I have power either to free you or to crucify you?"

[11] Jesus answered, "You would have no power over me if it were not given to you from above. Therefore the one who handed me over to you is guilty of a greater sin."

[12] From then on, Pilate tried to set Jesus free, but the Jews kept shouting, "If you let this man go, you are no friend of Caesar. Anyone who claims to be a king opposes Caesar."

[13] When Pilate heard this, he brought Jesus out and sat down on the judge's seat at a place known as the Stone Pavement (which in Aramaic is Gabbatha). [14] It was the day of Preparation of Passover Week, about the sixth hour.

"Here is your king," Pilate said to the Jews.

[15] But they shouted, "Take him away! Take him away! Crucify him!"

"Shall I crucify your king?" Pilate asked.

"We have no king but Caesar," the chief priests answered.

[16] Finally Pilate handed him over to them to be crucified.

The Crucifixion

So the soldiers took charge of Jesus. [17] Carrying his own cross, he went out to the place of the Skull (which in Aramaic is called Golgotha). [18] Here they crucified him, and with him two others — one on each side and Jesus in the middle.

[19] Pilate had a notice prepared and fastened to the cross. It read: JESUS OF NAZARETH, THE KING OF THE JEWS. [20] Many of the Jews read this sign, for the place where Jesus was crucified was near the city, and the sign was written in Aramaic, Latin and Greek. [21] The chief priests of the Jews protested to Pilate, "Do not write 'The King of the Jews,' but that this man claimed to be king of the Jews."

[22] Pilate answered, "What I have written, I have written."

[23] When the soldiers crucified Jesus, they took his clothes, dividing them into four shares, one for each of them, with the undergarment remaining. This garment was seamless, woven in one piece from top to bottom.

[24] "Let's not tear it," they said to one another. "Let's decide by lot who will get it."

This happened that the scripture might be fulfilled which said,

"They divided my garments among
them
and cast lots for my clothing."[a]

So this is what the soldiers did.

[25] Near the cross of Jesus stood his mother, his mother's sister, Mary the wife of Clopas, and Mary Magdalene. [26] When Jesus saw his mother there, and the disciple whom he loved standing nearby, he said to his mother, "Dear woman, here is

[a] 24 Psalm 22:18

your son," [27] and to the disciple, "Here is your mother." From that time on, this disciple took her into his home.

The Death of Jesus

[28] Later, knowing that all was now completed, and so that the Scripture would be fulfilled, Jesus said, "I am thirsty." [29] A jar of wine vinegar was there, so they soaked a sponge in it, put the sponge on a stalk of the hyssop plant, and lifted it to Jesus' lips. [30] When he had received the drink, Jesus said, "It is finished." With that, he bowed his head and gave up his spirit.

[31] Now it was the day of Preparation, and the next day was to be a special Sabbath. Because the Jews did not want the bodies left on the crosses during the Sabbath, they asked Pilate to have the legs broken and the bodies taken down. [32] The soldiers therefore came and broke the legs of the first man who had been crucified with Jesus, and then those of the other. [33] But when they came to Jesus and found that he was already dead, they did not break his legs. [34] Instead, one of the soldiers pierced Jesus' side with a spear, bringing a sudden flow of blood and water. [35] The man who saw it has given testimony, and his testimony is true. He knows that he tells the truth, and he testifies so that you also may believe. [36] These things happened so that the scripture would be fulfilled: "Not one of his bones will be broken,"[a] [37] and, as another scripture says, "They will look on the one they have pierced."[b]

The Burial of Jesus

[38] Later, Joseph of Arimathea asked Pilate for the body of Jesus. Now Joseph was a disciple of Jesus, but secretly because he feared the Jews. With Pilate's permission, he came and took the body away. [39] He was accompanied by Nicodemus, the man who earlier had visited Jesus at night. Nicodemus brought a mixture of myrrh and aloes, about seventy-five pounds.[c] [40] Taking Jesus' body, the two of them wrapped it, with the spices, in strips of linen. This was in accordance with Jewish burial customs. [41] At the place where Jesus was crucified, there was a garden, and in the garden a new tomb, in which no one had ever been laid. [42] Because it was the Jewish day of Preparation and since the tomb was nearby, they laid Jesus there.

The Empty Tomb

20 Early on the first day of the week, while it was still dark, Mary Magdalene went to the tomb and saw that the stone had been removed from the entrance. [2] So she came running to Simon Peter and the other disciple, the one Jesus loved, and said, "They have taken the Lord out of the tomb, and we don't know where they have put him!"

[3] So Peter and the other disciple started for the tomb. [4] Both were running, but the other disciple outran Peter and reached the tomb first. [5] He bent over and looked in at the strips of linen lying there but did not go in. [6] Then Simon Peter, who was behind

---

[a] 36 Exodus 12:46; Num. 9:12; Psalm 34:20   [b] 37 Zech. 12:10   [c] 39 Greek a hundred litrai (about 34 kilograms)

him, arrived and went into the tomb. He saw the strips of linen lying there, [7] as well as the burial cloth that had been around Jesus' head. The cloth was folded up by itself, separate from the linen. [8] Finally the other disciple, who had reached the tomb first, also went inside. He saw and believed. [9] (They still did not understand from Scripture that Jesus had to rise from the dead.)

Jesus Appears to Mary Magdalene

[10] Then the disciples went back to their homes, [11] but Mary stood outside the tomb crying. As she wept, she bent over to look into the tomb [12] and saw two angels in white, seated where Jesus' body had been, one at the head and the other at the foot.

[13] They asked her, "Woman, why are you crying?"

"They have taken my Lord away," she said, "and I don't know where they have put him." [14] At this, she turned around and saw Jesus standing there, but she did not realize that it was Jesus.

[15] "Woman," he said, "why are you crying? Who is it you are looking for?"

Thinking he was the gardener, she said, "Sir, if you have carried him away, tell me where you have put him, and I will get him."

[16] Jesus said to her, "Mary."

She turned toward him and cried out in Aramaic, "Rabboni!" (which means Teacher).

[17] Jesus said, "Do not hold on to me, for I have not yet returned to the Father. Go instead to my brothers and tell them, 'I am returning to my Father and your Father, to my God and your God.'"

[18] Mary Magdalene went to the disciples with the news: "I have seen the Lord!" And she told them that he had said these things to her.

Jesus Appears to His Disciples

[19] On the evening of that first day of the week, when the disciples were together, with the doors locked for fear of the Jews, Jesus came and stood among them and said, "Peace be with you!" [20] After he said this, he showed them his hands and side. The disciples were overjoyed when they saw the Lord.

[21] Again Jesus said, "Peace be with you! As the Father has sent me, I am sending you." [22] And with that he breathed on them and said, "Receive the Holy Spirit. [23] If you forgive anyone his sins, they are forgiven; if you do not forgive them, they are not forgiven."

Jesus Appears to Thomas

[24] Now Thomas (called Didymus), one of the Twelve, was not with the disciples when Jesus came. [25] So the other disciples told him, "We have seen the Lord!"

But he said to them, "Unless I see the nail marks in his hands and put my finger where the nails were, and put my hand into his side, I will not believe it."

[26] A week later his disciples were in the house again, and Thomas was with them. Though the doors were locked, Jesus came and stood among them and said, "Peace be with you!" [27] Then he said to Thomas, "Put your finger here; see my hands. Reach

out your hand and put it into my side. Stop doubting and believe."

²⁸ Thomas said to him, "My Lord and my God!"

²⁹ Then Jesus told him, "Because you have seen me, you have believed; blessed are those who have not seen and yet have believed."

³⁰ Jesus did many other miraculous signs in the presence of his disciples, which are not recorded in this book. ³¹ But these are written that you may*ᵃ* believe that Jesus is the Christ, the Son of God, and that by believing you may have life in his name.

Jesus and the Miraculous Catch of Fish

21 Afterward Jesus appeared again to his disciples, by the Sea of Tiberias.*ᵇ* It happened this way: ² Simon Peter, Thomas (called Didymus), Nathanael from Cana in Galilee, the sons of Zebedee, and two other disciples were together. ³ "I'm going out to fish," Simon Peter told them, and they said, "We'll go with you." So they went out and got into the boat, but that night they caught nothing.

⁴ Early in the morning, Jesus stood on the shore, but the disciples did not realize that it was Jesus.

⁵ He called out to them, "Friends, haven't you any fish?"

"No," they answered.

⁶ He said, "Throw your net on the right side of the boat and you will find some." When they did, they were unable to haul the net in because of the large number of fish.

⁷ Then the disciple whom Jesus loved said to Peter, "It is the Lord!" As soon as Simon Peter heard him say, "It is the Lord," he wrapped his outer garment around him (for he had taken it off) and jumped into the water. ⁸ The other disciples followed in the boat, towing the net full of fish, for they were not far from shore, about a hundred yards.*ᶜ* ⁹ When they landed, they saw a fire of burning coals there with fish on it, and some bread.

¹⁰ Jesus said to them, "Bring some of the fish you have just caught."

¹¹ Simon Peter climbed aboard and dragged the net ashore. It was full of large fish, 153, but even with so many the net was not torn. ¹² Jesus said to them, "Come and have breakfast." None of the disciples dared ask him, "Who are you?" They knew it was the Lord. ¹³ Jesus came, took the bread and gave it to them, and did the same with the fish. ¹⁴ This was now the third time Jesus appeared to his disciples after he was raised from the dead.

Jesus Reinstates Peter

¹⁵ When they had finished eating, Jesus said to Simon Peter, "Simon son of John, do you truly love me more than these?"

"Yes, Lord," he said, "you know that I love you."

Jesus said, "Feed my lambs."

¹⁶ Again Jesus said, "Simon son of John, do you truly love me?"

He answered, "Yes, Lord, you know that I love you."

Jesus said, "Take care of my sheep."

ᵃ 31 Some manuscripts *may continue to*   *ᵇ 1* That is, Sea of Galilee   *ᶜ 8* Greek *about two hundred* cubits (about 90 meters)

[17] The third time he said to him, "Simon son of John, do you love me?"

Peter was hurt because Jesus asked him the third time, "Do you love me?" He said, "Lord, you know all things; you know that I love you."

Jesus said, "Feed my sheep. [18] I tell you the truth, when you were younger you dressed yourself and went where you wanted; but when you are old you will stretch out your hands, and someone else will dress you and lead you where you do not want to go." [19] Jesus said this to indicate the kind of death by which Peter would glorify God. Then he said to him, "Follow me!"

[20] Peter turned and saw that the disciple whom Jesus loved was following them. (This was the one who had leaned back against Jesus at the supper and had said, "Lord, who is going to betray you?") [21] When Peter saw him, he asked, "Lord, what about him?"

[22] Jesus answered, "If I want him to remain alive until I return, what is that to you? You must follow me." [23] Because of this, the rumor spread among the brothers that this disciple would not die. But Jesus did not say that he would not die; he only said, "If I want him to remain alive until I return, what is that to you?"

[24] This is the disciple who testifies to these things and who wrote them down. We know that his testimony is true.

[25] Jesus did many other things as well. If every one of them were written down, I suppose that even the whole world would not have room for the books that would be written.

ABOUT THE
NIV

ABOUT THE
NEW INTERNATIONAL VERSION

THE NEW INTERNATIONAL VERSION is a completely new translation of the Holy Bible made by over a hundred scholars working directly from the best available Hebrew, Aramaic and Greek texts. It had its beginning in 1965 when, after several years of exploratory study by committees from the Christian Reformed Church and the National Association of Evangelicals, a group of scholars met at Palos Heights, Illinois, and concurred in the need for a new translation of the Bible in contemporary English. This group, though not made up of official church representatives, was transdenominational. Its conclusion was endorsed by a large number of leaders from many denominations who met in Chicago in 1966.

Responsibility for the new version was delegated by the Palos Heights group to a self-governing body of fifteen, the Committee on Bible Translation, composed for the most part of biblical scholars from colleges, universities and seminaries. In 1967 the New York Bible Society (then the International Bible Society and now Biblica, Inc.™) generously undertook the financial sponsorship of the project — a sponsorship that made it possible to enlist the help of many distinguished scholars. The fact that participants from the United States,

Great Britain, Canada, Australia and New Zealand worked together gave the project its international scope. That they were from many denominations — including Anglican, Assemblies of God, Baptist, Brethren, Christian Reformed, Church of Christ, Evangelical Free, Lutheran, Mennonite, Methodist, Nazarene, Presbyterian, Wesleyan and other churches — helped to safeguard the translation from sectarian bias.

How it was made helps to give the New International Version its distinctiveness. The translation of each book was assigned to a team of scholars. Next, one of the Intermediate Editorial Committees revised the initial translation, with constant reference to the Hebrew, Aramaic or Greek. Their work then went to one of the General Editorial Committees, which checked it in detail and made another thorough revision. This revision in turn was carefully reviewed by the Committee on Bible Translation, which made further changes and then released the final version for publication. In this way the entire Bible underwent three revisions, during each of which the translation was examined for its faithfulness to the original languages and for its English style.

All this involved many thousands of

hours of research and discussion regarding the meaning of the texts and the precise way of putting them into English. It may well be that no other translation has been made by a more thorough process of review and revision from committee to committee than this one.

From the beginning of the project, the Committee on Bible Translation held to certain goals for the New International Version: that it would be an accurate translation and one that would have clarity and literary quality and so prove suitable for public and private reading, teaching, preaching, memorizing and liturgical use. The Committee also sought to preserve some measure of continuity with the long tradition of translating the Scriptures into English.

In working toward these goals, the translators were united in their commitment to the authority and infallibility of the Bible as God's Word in written form. They believe that it contains the divine answer to the deepest needs of humanity, that it sheds unique light on our path in a dark world, and that it sets forth the way to our eternal well-being.

The first concern of the translators has been the accuracy of the translation and its fidelity to the thought of the biblical writers. They have weighed the significance of the lexical and grammatical details of the Hebrew, Aramaic and Greek texts. At the same time, they have striven for more than a word-for-word translation. Because thought patterns and syntax differ from language to language, faithful communication of the meaning of the writers of the Bible demands frequent modifications in sentence structure and constant regard for the contextual meanings of words.

A sensitive feeling for style does not always accompany scholarship. Accordingly the Committee on Bible Translation submitted the developing version to a number of stylistic consultants. Two of them read every book of both Old and New Testaments twice — once before and once after the last major revision — and made invaluable suggestions. Samples of the translation were tested for clarity and ease of reading by various kinds of people — young and old, highly educated and less well educated, ministers and laymen.

Concern for clear and natural English — that the New International Version should be idiomatic but not idiosyncratic, contemporary but not dated — motivated the translators and consultants. At the same time, they tried to reflect the differing styles of the biblical writers. In view of the international use of English, the translators sought to avoid obvious Americanisms on the one hand and obvious Anglicisms on the other. A British edition reflects the comparatively few differences of significant idiom and of spelling.

As for the traditional pronouns "thou," "thee" and "thine" in reference to the Deity, the translators judged that to use these archaisms (along with the old verb forms such as "doest," "wouldest" and "hadst") would violate accuracy in translation. Neither Hebrew, Aramaic nor Greek uses special pronouns for the persons of the Godhead. A present-day translation is not enhanced by forms that in the time of the

King James Version were used in everyday speech, whether referring to God or man.

For the Old Testament the standard Hebrew text, the Masoretic Text as published in the latest editions of *Biblia Hebraica,* was used throughout. The Dead Sea Scrolls contain material bearing on an earlier stage of the Hebrew text. They were consulted, as were the Samaritan Pentateuch and the ancient scribal traditions relating to textual changes. Sometimes a variant Hebrew reading in the margin of the Masoretic Text was followed instead of the text itself. Such instances, being variants within the Masoretic tradition, are not specified by footnotes. In rare cases, words in the consonantal text were divided differently from the way they appear in the Masoretic Text. Footnotes indicate this. The translators also consulted the more important early versions — the Septuagint; Aquila, Symmachus and Theodotion; the Vulgate; the Syriac Peshitta; the Targums; and for the Psalms the *Juxta Hebraica* of Jerome. Readings from these versions were occasionally followed where the Masoretic Text seemed doubtful and where accepted principles of textual criticism showed that one or more of these textual witnesses appeared to provide the correct reading. Such instances are footnoted. Sometimes vowel letters and vowel signs did not, in the judgment of the translators, represent the correct vowels for the original consonantal text. Accordingly some words were read with a different set of vowels. These instances are usually not indicated by footnotes.

The Greek text used in translating the New Testament was an eclectic one. No other piece of ancient literature has such an abundance of manuscript witnesses as does the New Testament. Where existing manuscripts differ, the translators made their choice of readings according to accepted principles of New Testament textual criticism. Footnotes call attention to places where there was uncertainty about what the original text was. The best current printed texts of the Greek New Testament were used.

There is a sense in which the work of translation is never wholly finished. This applies to all great literature and uniquely so to the Bible. In 1973 the New Testament in the New International Version was published. Since then, suggestions for corrections and revisions have been received from various sources. The Committee on Bible Translation carefully considered the suggestions and adopted a number of them. These were incorporated in the first printing of the entire Bible in 1978. Additional revisions were made by the Committee on Bible Translation in 1983 and appear in printings after that date.

As in other ancient documents, the precise meaning of the biblical texts is sometimes uncertain. This is more often the case with the Hebrew and Aramaic texts than with the Greek text. Although archaeological and linguistic discoveries in this century aid in understanding difficult passages, some uncertainties remain. The more significant of these have been called to the reader's attention in the footnotes.

In regard to the divine name *YHWH,* commonly referred to as the *Tetragram-*

maton, the translators adopted the device used in most English versions of rendering that name as "LORD" in capital letters to distinguish it from *Adonai,* another Hebrew word rendered "Lord," for which small letters are used. Wherever the two names stand together in the Old Testament as a compound name of God, they are rendered "Sovereign LORD."

Because for most readers today the phrases "the LORD of hosts" and "God of hosts" have little meaning, this version renders them "the LORD Almighty" and "God Almighty." These renderings convey the sense of the Hebrew, namely, "he who is sovereign over all the 'hosts' (powers) in heaven and on earth, especially over the 'hosts' (armies) of Israel." For readers unacquainted with Hebrew this does not make clear the distinction between *Sabaoth* ("hosts" or "Almighty") and *Shaddai* (which can also be translated "Almighty"), but the latter occurs infrequently and is always footnoted. When *Adonai* and *YHWH Sabaoth* occur together, they are rendered "the Lord, the LORD Almighty."

As for other proper nouns, the familiar spellings of the King James Version are generally retained. Names traditionally spelled with "ch," except where it is final, are usually spelled in this translation with "k" or "c," since the biblical languages do not have the sound that "ch" frequently indicates in English — for example, in *chant.* For well-known names such as Zechariah, however, the traditional spelling has been retained. Variation in the spelling of names in the original languages has usually not been indicated. Where a person or place has two or more different names in the Hebrew, Aramaic or Greek texts, the more familiar one has generally been used, with footnotes where needed.

To achieve clarity the translators sometimes supplied words not in the original texts but required by the context. If there was uncertainty about such material, it is enclosed in brackets. Also for the sake of clarity or style, nouns, including some proper nouns, are sometimes substituted for pronouns, and vice versa. And though the Hebrew writers often shifted back and forth between first, second and third personal pronouns without change of antecedent, this translation often makes them uniform, in accordance with English style and without the use of footnotes.

Poetical passages are printed as poetry, that is, with indentation of lines and with separate stanzas. These are generally designed to reflect the structure of Hebrew poetry. This poetry is normally characterized by parallelism in balanced lines. Most of the poetry in the Bible is in the Old Testament, and scholars differ regarding the scansion of Hebrew lines. The translators determined the stanza divisions for the most part by analysis of the subject matter. The stanzas therefore serve as poetic paragraphs.

As an aid to the reader, italicized sectional headings are inserted in most of the books. They are not to be regarded as part of the NIV text, are not for oral reading, and are not intended to dictate the interpretation of the sections they head.

The footnotes in this version are of several kinds, most of which need no explanation. Those giving alternative translations begin with "Or" and generally introduce the alternative with the last word preceding it in the text, except when it is a single-word alternative; in poetry quoted in a footnote a slant mark indicates a line division. Footnotes introduced by "Or" do not have uniform significance. In some cases two possible translations were considered to have about equal validity. In other cases, though the translators were convinced that the translation in the text was correct, they judged that another interpretation was possible and of sufficient importance to be represented in a footnote.

In the New Testament, footnotes that refer to uncertainty regarding the original text are introduced by "Some manuscripts" or similar expressions. In the Old Testament, evidence for the reading chosen is given first and evidence for the alternative is added after a semicolon (for example: Septuagint; Hebrew *father*). In such notes the term "Hebrew" refers to the Masoretic Text.

It should be noted that minerals, flora and fauna, architectural details, articles of clothing and jewelry, musical instruments and other articles cannot always be identified with precision. Also measures of capacity in the biblical period are particularly uncertain (see the table of weights and measures following the text).

Like all translations of the Bible, made as they are by imperfect man, this one undoubtedly falls short of its goals. Yet we are grateful to God for the extent to which he has enabled us to realize these goals and for the strength he has given us and our colleagues to complete our task. We offer this version of the Bible to him in whose name and for whose glory it has been made. We pray that it will lead many into a better understanding of the Holy Scriptures and a fuller knowledge of Jesus Christ the incarnate Word, of whom the Scriptures so faithfully testify.

The Committee on Bible Translation

June 1978
(Revised August 1983)

Names of the translators and editors
may be secured from Biblica, Inc.™,
translation sponsors of the New International Version,
1820 Jet Stream Drive, Colorado Springs, Colorado
80921 – 3696 U.S.A.

MEET
LEE STROBEL